THE PLOTTERS OF
CABBAGE PATCH CORNER

A Musical Play

Book, Music and Lyrics by
DAVID WOOD

SAMUEL FRENCH

LONDON

NEW YORK SYDNEY TORONTO HOLLYWOOD

AUTHOR'S NOTE

This play was written especially for children's audiences, and therefore should be played for real, with no concessions to adult innuendo. It has been found essential in production that the "pretties" and the "uglies" should be well balanced. The battle in the garden is not between "goodies" and "baddies"—both sides have a legitimate point of view. It is perfectly normal, and indeed desirable, that the audience should take opposite sides in the participation, but the arguments should be presented clearly enough for them to unite, with the insects, by the end. The play was not written as an ecological tract! It is simply a story about the problems confronting a group of insects, and the ways in which they try to sort them out. Played with sincerity, it should involve the audience and encourage them to think about and discuss the various attitudes it depicts. It goes without saying that the humour and excitement should be brought out as much as possible, as long as it relates directly to character and situation.

DAVID WOOD

THE PLOTTERS OF CABBAGE PATCH CORNER

First presented by the Worcester Repertory Company at the Swan Theatre, Worcester, on 26 December 1970, with the following cast of characters:

Glow Worm	*Dan Jones*
Ladybird	*Marcia King*
Ant	*Don Dryden*
Slug	*David Sadgrove*
Red Admiral	*Richard Carrington*
Greenfly	*Alison Steadman*
Maggot	*Jill Lidstone*
Bumble Bee	*John A. Cooper*
The Great Mushroom	*Peter Wickham*
Spider	*Jean Heywood*

The play directed by **Mick Hughes**

Designed by **Richard Hammond**

Musical director: **Philip Wilby**

The play was subsequently produced by Eddie Kulukundis for Knightsbridge Theatrical Productions Ltd., & W.S.G. Productions Ltd., at the Shaw Theatre, London, on 15 December 1971, with the following cast:

Glow Worm	*Robert McBain*
Ladybird	*Julia McKenzie*
Ant	*Maurice Lane*
Slug	*Timothy Davies*
Red Admiral	*Ben Aris*
Greenfly	*Bridget Turner*
Maggot	*Apple Brook*
Bumble Bee	*Norman Warwick*
The Great Mushroom	*Paul McDowell*
Spider	*Sandra Shipley*

The play directed by **Jonathan Lynn**

Designed by **Susie Caulcutt**

Musical director: **Peter Pontzen**

The action of the play takes place in a garden

Time: the present.

The music for this play is available from Samuel French Ltd.

DESCRIPTION OF CHARACTERS

Glow Worm	Elderly, short-sighted, well-meaning
Ladybird	Middle-aged, efficient, quite attractive but smug
Ant	Speedy, offhand though not unfriendly, abrupt, his work is all to him
Slug	Oily and villainous
Red Admiral	Retired Naval Officer, pipe smoking, enthusiastic organizer
Greenfly	Rather vulgar, loud-mouthed, undignified
Maggot	Naughty boy, cry baby, greedy, a stammerer
Bumble Bee	Practical, pleasant, business-like
The Great Mushroom	The Oracle. After a big build-up, he should be a funny anti-climax: his bad cold should help
Spider	Old, a bit frightening, witchlike
The Big Ones	The voices of the Man and Woman should be live, over loudspeakers

DESCRIPTION OF THE SET

This is a garden, and should naturally be on a large scale because the characters are insects. Flowers, Slug's cabbage, Ladybird's leaf, Ant's flower, etc. could be permanent. The compost heap, Spider's house, Red Admiral's cocoon, etc., could be on trucks. The final important transformation should incorporate large sunflowers growing at the back.

MUSICAL NUMBERS

ACT I*

SCENE 1

A garden

We hear the dawn chorus as the Curtain rises—the dim lighting on the garden increases as dawn breaks

Glow Worm enters with his lantern, bag, and "Insect News"

Glow Worm (*singing*)   **1**

   Here comes the morning
   I can see the sun,
   A new day is dawning
   And there's work to be done.

He goes to Ladybird's leaf and knocks

   Time to get up
   Time to get up
   Time to get up.

Ladybird enters

Ladybird Good morning, Glow Worm.
Glow Worm Good morning, Ladybird. Sleep well?
Ladybird (*stretching*) Yes, thank you.
Glow Worm Here's your paper. (*He gives her the leaf-shaped "Insect News"*)
Ladybird Thank you. Any disturbances in the garden last night?
Glow Worm No. I had a very quiet watch. (*He yawns, turning away from her*) And now I could do with a snooze.
Ladybird (*turning his chin to her*) Don't forget the meeting!
Glow Worm I'll be there, and I'll try not to fall asleep this time!
Ladybird It's going to be a lovely day, I think.
Glow Worm Let's hope so. I must carry on with my rounds.

Glow Worm and Ladybird sing

Together   Here comes the morning

---

*N.B. Paragraph 3 on page ii of this Acting Edition regarding photocopying and video-recording should be carefully read.

Ladybird	Ev'ry bluebell rings.
Together	A new day is dawning
Ladybird	Open your eyes—stretch your wings
Glow Worm	Time to get up.

Ladybird (*speaking*) I must polish my spots and get ready. (*She goes into her leaf and emerges with a mirror, leaving the "News" inside*)

Glow Worm (*singing*)

Time to get up. (*He stops by a flower*)
Time to get up.

Ant enters through the flower

Ant Good gracious, morning already? Where's my wheelbarrow? (*He goes to the wheelbarrow*) Where's my wheelbarrow? Hurry scurry, hurry scurry. Morning, Glow Worm.

Glow Worm Good morning, Ant.

Ant (*pushing past with the wheelbarrow*) Excuse me. No time to be lost. It's all hurry scurry, very busy today — food to fetch for the Queen Mother *and* all the workers—they're spring cleaning the anthill this week. Hurry scurry, hurry scurry. Morning, Ladybird.

Ant exits with the wheelbarrow

Ladybird (*as he goes*) Good morning, Ant. Don't forget the meeting . . . Oh, he's gone.

Ladybird exits under her leaf

Glow Worm (*singing*)

Here comes the morning
I can see the sun.
A new day is dawning
And there's work to be done.

Time to get up
Time to get up (*He moves to the cabbage*)
Time to get up.

(*Speaking*) Come along, you lazy slug.

Slug emerges from the cabbage, crawling with a stick

Slug What is it, Glow Worm?
Glow Worm Time to get up for the meeting.
Slug Oh! Any letters for me?
Glow Worm Not this morning

Glow Worm exits

SONG: SLUG'S SONG   2

Slug (*Yawn, yawn*)
      Getting up is hard
      For a sleepy slug, ug, ug, ug,
      In my cabbage
      I was snug as a bug in a rug, ug, ug.

      But a new day is dawning,
      I must glide out of hiding—
      Stop dithering,
      And into the morning
      Go sliding
      And slithering;
      (*Yawn, yawn*)
      But getting up is hard
      For a sleepy slug, ug, ug, **ug.**
      In my cabbage
      I was snug as a bug in a rug,
      Ug, Ug, Ug,
      Ug, Ug, Ug, Ug.

   Red Admiral enters from his cocoon

Red Admiral (*Heartily, slapping Slug on the back*) What ho! Toodly pip.
   (*He prods Slug with his foot*) Morning, Slug.
Slug Morning, Red Admiral.
Red Admiral Where's the rest of the crew? Meeting on deck any mo, you
   know. Where's the Secretary?
Slug Do you have to be so hearty at this time of the morning? Ladybird's
   getting ready, I expect.
Red Admiral Ah! Top hole—still in her cabin, I dare say. (*He goes to the
   leaf*) My, what a lovely morning! (*He knocks on the leaf and goes in*)
   Ladybird, shake a leg there.

   Red Admiral exits behind the leaf

Slug Ugghh. (*He continues his song*)
   (*Singing*) Gosh
         I need a wash,
         I mustn't look grimy—
         Just a little bit slimy,
         Make my tentacles look tidy and spruce;
         I need
         A breakfast feed—
         A slice of hollyhock and a cup of cabbage juice.
         (*Yawn, yawn*)
         But getting up is hard
         For a sleepy slug, ug, ug, ug.
         In my cabbage
         I was snug as a bug in a rug,

Ug, ug, ug,
Ug, ug.
Ug, ug.
(*He lies by the cabbage with his leg up and falls asleep*)

Greenfly enters quickly, hand outstretched as if holding something; she doesn't see Slug but trips over his foot, falling over

Greenfly (*getting up*) Ooh, I was sure I was going to be late, and what happens? I arrive and there's nobody here—maybe they've all overslept. There's no-one here at all!

The Audience should shout out that someone is there. Greenfly reacts accordingly—eventually seeing Slug

Ooh! It's Slug—fast asleep—ooh, he's a lazy old thing, he really is. I'd better not wake him up—he can be very nasty sometimes—so I'll wait till the meeting starts. Now, I'm Greenfly, and this is my . . . (*She becomes aware that something is missing from her outstretched hand*) 'Ere—well, I never. He's gone again—that little boy of mine. I take my eyes off him for half a jiffy and now he's hopped off. (*Calling*) Maggot! *Maggot!* (*To the Audience*) You haven't seen my little boy, Maggot, have you? He's sort of small and a dirty off-white colour—

Maggot enters from above the cabbage, unseen by Greenfly

The Audience shout out

—and *very* naughty and . . .

Wherever the Audience points to, Maggot goes somewhere else, so that Greenfly, getting more and more annoyed and pretending that the Audience are playing a trick on her, cannot see Maggot

Eventually Maggot exits, and Greenfly looks all round

(*To the Audience*) Ooh. You're so naughty, He's not there at all. You've been fooling me all this time, etc. (*She carries on talking ad lib.*)

Maggot drags on a large Green Pea, which he starts rolling towards Greenfly, slowly, and without her knowing. When it's near her he makes a noise, causing her to turn suddenly and bump into or even fall under the rolling pea

What's that?
Maggot (*laughing loudly*) A pppea, I pppinched it from a pppod.
Greenfly (*getting up; crossly*) Maggot, you naughty boy—come here.
Maggot Sh, sh, shan't. (*He puts his tongue out*)
Greenfly Ssh, you'll wake Uncle Slug.
Maggot Don't care.
Greenfly (*starting to advance*) Mummy get cross.
Maggot Mummy always cross.

They start going round the pea in a circle, Maggot dodging away from Greenfly

Greenfly She isn't.
Maggot She is.
Greenfly She isn't.
Maggot She is.
Greenfly (*pointing*) Ooh look, Maggot, a big juicy apple . . .
Maggot (*turning around*) Where? I just fffancy a bbbite of apple.

Greenfly creeps round behind the pea. Maggot turns and faces the pea again; he notices Greenfly has gone

Where's she gone?

Greenfly appears round the other side of the pea, grabs Maggot and smacks his bottom

Greenfly Got you—you're a bad, bad maggot.

Maggot screams in pain and anger, waking up Slug

Slug What's that nasty sound? (*He sees Maggot*) Cease your noise, Maggot —I was dreaming a delicious dream about a cos lettuce—and you woke me up just as I started munching . . .
Greenfly Sorry, Slug. Maggot, apologize to Uncle Slug.
Maggot Sh, sh, shan't.
Greenfly Do as you're told.
Maggot Sh, sh, shan't. (*He puts his tongue out at Slug*)
Slug My word, what a rude maggot you are.
Greenfly You naughty boy . . .

There is a general row, broken by the appearance of Red Admiral and Lady-bird from the leaf

Ladybird Oh dear, what's going on?
Red Admiral Trouble in the ranks.

Red Admiral blows his whistle very loudly, his wings go up. The others shuffle to attention as if through habit

Red Admiral Thank you. At ease.

All relax. Red Admiral takes out his pocket watch

The time is precisely seven-hundred hours—prepare for the Insects' Committee Meeting.

SONG: THE INSECT COMMITTEE   3

Maggot rolls the pea off, and Slug exits above the cabbage

All   The Insect Committee sits once a week
                 When ev'ry insect who's of age is free to speak

> We deal with insect matters whether large or small
> From the Insect Welfare Clinic to the Ugly Bug Ball.

*As the song proceeds the five characters prepare for the meeting, setting a
barrel, toadstools or acorn cups to sit on. Ant brings a map. Slug enters with
a table, and Maggot helps, or hinders, him in setting it up. Ladybird collects
a book and pencil from her leaf for the minutes. Slug fetches a cup of cabbage
juice and a slice of hollyhock from his cabbage home*

> The Insect Committee knows what to do
> If daddy long legs has a broken leg or two
> We punish naughty earwigs who attack and rob.
> If a beetle's out of work we'll help him find a new job.
>
> We pass insect laws
> In the public insect cause.
> We don't suffer insect fools—
> We run public insect schools.
>
> Ladybird is very
> Good as secretary.
> She takes all the minutes—

Ladybird   There's really nothing in it.
Red Admiral And I take the chair.
All   He takes the chair
> Admiral takes the chair
>
> We feel so responsible—it's not funny
> Voting how to spend the public insect money.
> If we don't run the garden the efficient way
> (The) Nat'nal Union of Insects will have something to say.
>
> The Insect Committee sits once a week.
> When ev'ry insect who's of age is free to speak.
> We deal with insect matters whether large or small—
> From the Insect Welfare Clinic to the Ugly Bug Ball.

*As the song ends they sit, Red Admiral in the centre, Maggot then Slug to
R of him, Ladybird then Greenfly to his L. Red Admiral opens the map and
bangs on the table with his pipe*

Red Admiral I declare this meeting well and truly launched. We will, if the
Secretary agrees, take the minutes as read.

Ladybird nods with agreement

And pass to . . .

Slug makes loud slurping noises as he drinks his juice

Slug, do you have to?

Slug What?

Red Admiral Make that undisciplined noise.

Slug What noise? (*He drinks again, making the same noise*)

Red Admiral *That* noise.

Slug I'm sorry. I'm only having my breakfast. (*He makes the noise again*)

Maggot Can I have a bite of hollyhock, Uncle Slug? (*He holds out his hand*)

Slug No. Keep your grubby paws off. (*He slaps Maggot's hand*)

Greenfly That's right, Slug. You tell him.

Maggot I want some.

Slug No!

Maggot Yes!

Slug No!

Ladybird (*tapping firmly with her pencil*) Order, please. We have business to attend to.

Slug Just let him touch my hollyhock, that's all.

Red Admiral Now come along. Stop squalling.

Slug (*to the Audience*) If he touches it, just let me know, please, eh?

Red Admiral Now, first on today's agenda, there is the—

Maggot starts advancing on the hollyhock

—important question of—

The Audience should start shouting. Slug just catches Maggot in time. Maggot retreats. Red Admiral keeps talking all through this as if nothing is happening, improvising if necessary

—the problem we have been facing for quite a long time now—the question which I know we are all longing to discuss in detail—

Maggot's advancing business is repeated several times, till finally he gets the hollyhock slice away from Slug and holds it away from him—under Red Admiral's fist

—and that is *whether* . . . (*On this word Red Admiral's fist comes down to make the point—it squelches into the hollyhock slice*) Ugh! Oh, no. Maggot, that's enough. Greenfly, kindly control your horrible child immediately.

Ladybird hands a handkerchief to Greenfly, who passes it to Red Admiral. Slug puts down his cup and grabs Maggot

Slug You wretched grub. (*He shakes Maggot*) That was my last slice.

Greenfly gets up and drags Maggot back to her seat

Greenfly Come over here this minute.

Maggot Ow!

Red Admiral's wings go up and he blows his whistle. All stiffen to attention

Red Admiral Thank you. At ease! (*His wings go down*) Ladybird, if you navigate yourself to over there (*indicating where Maggot was*) and if Greenfly docked there (*indicating where Ladybird was*)—we could get some work done.

Ladybird Of course, Admiral. (*She takes her book and sits next to Red Admiral*)

Greenfly sits where Ladybird was, keeping an eye on Maggot

Red Admiral (*looking round to see that all is still*) Good—plain sailing from now on, let's hope. As I was saying, the question of the Old Insects Home. As you know—(*indicating the map*)—the Old Insects Home is located here by the rhubarb—fifty-five longitude, eighty-four latitude—an ideal spot for elderly insects—faces south and is well protected by the garden fence to the north-west—here. Over to you, Ladybird.

Ladybird The proposal is that, because the Home is becoming overcrowded with old insects we should ask the ants to build a new wing.

Red Admiral So, could we please vote—those in favour.

All but Maggot raise their hands. Greenfly nudges Maggot and makes him hold his hand up

At this moment Ant enters, his wheelbarrow full

Ah! Ant, just in time, we're voting for a new wing for the Old Insects Home to be built by you and your fellow workers.

Ant (*putting down the barrow*) Well, we are very busy at the moment—new orders can't be carried out for some weeks. It's all hurry scurry, hurry scurry.

Ladybird Please, Ant . . .

Ant Oh! Very well, no time to argue. (*He raises his hand and immediately starts to exit*) But it can't be done immediately—so much to do and so little time, hurry scurry, hurry scurry.

Ant picks up the barrow and exits

Red Admiral Carried unanimously.

All take their hands down and clap and cheer

Now let's cruise on to the second point on today's agenda, the . . .   3a

We hear the sound of a back door opening. The lights dim and shadows of human legs are seen. Then human voices are heard above the stage. The Insects look up

Man (*off*) Come along, darling, let's have a look at the garden.

Woman (*off*) All right, dear, but don't get your feet muddy.

The Insects are listening. Then Slug, Greenfly and Maggot react terrified and scatter, eventually hiding by the leaf and the cabbage—Slug to the latter. All are still visible, however. Red Admiral and Ladybird stay where they are, adopting pretty poses

Man (*off*) Ah! Look, there's our beautiful butterfly.

Red Admiral looks pleased with himself

Woman (*off*) And there's that pretty ladybird, too.

Ladybird looks delighted and shows off her wings

Man (*off; furiously*) Look! There's that horrible slug.
Woman (*off*) And that ghastly greenfly.
Man (*off*) And that nasty little maggot. Take that.

We hear the SSSS of an aerosol spray and see perhaps through lighting or a snake effect, the spray attacking Slug, Greenfly and Maggot, who try to avoid it

Let's hope that's got rid of them. Pests, they ruin the garden—they eat all the plants . . .
Woman (*off*) And the vegetables.
Man (*off*) Come on, let's go in.

We hear the back door slam. Lights return to normal. Slug, Greenfly and Maggot return to the meeting

Red Admiral (*as though nothing much had happened*) Right, to return to business.
Slug Wait a minute, Admiral—I've got something to say first.
Greenfly So have I.
Maggot So have I.
Slug
Greenfly } Be quiet!
Red Admiral Very well, steam ahead.
Ladybird Should I note this down, Admiral?
Red Admiral I think you'd better.
Slug We're fed up.
Greenfly Fed up.
Maggot Fed up.
Slug
Greenfly } Be quiet!
Slug We're fed up with being sprayed by the Big Ones
Greenfly—sprayed by the Big Ones.
Maggot—sprayed by the Big Ones.
Slug
Greenfly } Be quiet!

SONG: INSECTICIDE   4

Slug ⎤	We're sitting in the sunshine
Greenfly ⎬	To pass the time of day
Maggot ⎦	When suddenly the Big Ones
	Get out their anti-insect spray
	And they go:
Chorus	SSSSS SSSSS
	Insecticide

SSSSS SSSSS
We run to hide
SSSSS SSSSS
Insecticide—
We nearly died
From insecticide.

Slug ⎫
Greenfly ⎬ We're walking in the garden
Maggot ⎭ Not breaking any law
When suddenly the Big Ones
Come running out of their back door
And they go:

Chorus   SSSSS SSSSS, etc.
(*The chorus is sung again twice*)

Oh yeah!

Red Admiral I'm sorry, shipmates—
Slug What d'you mean, I'm sorry shipmates?
Red Admiral—there's nothing this committee can do.
Ladybird We only deal with Insect Affairs—not the affairs of the Big Ones.
Greenfly But it's all right for you—they don't spray you.
Red Admiral That is hardly the point, Greenfly, We have no control over the Big Ones, and you know it, and, to be quite honest with you, you three do tend to do quite a bit of damage in the garden.
Ladybird Yes, one can see the Big Ones' point of view.
Greenfly Well I can't.
Slug Nor can I.
Maggot Nor can I.
All Be quiet.
Greenfly (*to Ladybird and Red Admiral*) Don't you tell my son to be quiet—it's difficult enough as it is, trying to bring him up properly. With all this spraying, it's so dangerous it's not safe to take him out any more.
Slug The time has come to act. The Big Ones must be taught a lesson.
Greenfly ⎫
Maggot ⎬ Hear, hear!
Slug No more spraying.
Greenfly ⎫
Maggot ⎬ Hear, hear!
Greenfly No more terrorizing innocent insects.
Slug ⎫
Maggot ⎬ Hear, hear!
Maggot And lots of food for growing maggots.
Slug ⎫
Greenfly ⎬ Hear, hear!

Red Admiral blows his whistle for silence

Slug Ha ha, that won't work any more, Admiral. We're not going to listen to you or your whistles again.

Greenfly (*to Ladybird*) Or you.
Ladybird Why not?
Slug You like the Big Ones.
Maggot And we don't.

Slug, Greenfly and Maggot clasp hands with one another in turn

SONG: DOWN WITH THE BIG ONES!   5

During the song, Slug, Maggot and Greenfly go off and collect banners with slogans on them, which they display

Greenfly ⎤
Slug　　 ⎬ Down with the Big Ones!
Maggot ⎦ Up, Resistance Underground!
　　　　　　 Down with the Big Ones!
　　　　　　 Down, down, down.
　　　　　　 Teach them a lesson!
　　　　　　 Make their garden look a sight!
　　　　　　 Down with the Big Ones—
　　　　　　 Fight, fight, fight.

Slug (*speaking*) Well. Are you with us, Admiral?
Red Admiral Certainly not.

(*He sings*)　　 The Big Ones like me
　　　　　　 For the rich colours I parade.
　　　　　　 It's no surprise
　　　　　　 That butterflies
　　　　　　 Are never sprayed.

Greenfly (*speaking*) What about you, Ladybird?
Ladybird (*singing*) The Big Ones like me

　　　　　　 For my spots and my pretty wings
　　　　　　 And if I land
　　　　　　 Upon their hand
　　　　　　 Good luck it brings.

Slug　　 ⎤
Greenfly ⎬ Down with the Big Ones, etc.
Maggot ⎦

As the chorus is sung, Bumble Bee enters with his ladder, which he leans against a plant and climbs

Slug There's Bumble Bee!
Greenfly Are you going to join us, Bumble Bee?
Bumble Bee Join you in what?
Maggot Down with the Big Ones!
Slug You must go on strike.
Bumble Bee Go on strike? If I did, the flowers would never get pollinated.
Slug Exactly.

Bumble Bee Oh no! I could never do that. The Big Ones have never done me any harm.

   (*He sings*)   The Big Ones like me:
                          But for me, flow'rs they wouldn't see.
                          I also store
                          The honey for
                          The Big Ones' tea.

During the next chorus, Slug, Greenfly and Maggot form in procession and move round the stage

   As they sing, Glow Worm enters with his lantern, returning home to bed: he automatically joins in Slug's procession. At the end of the chorus he stands with Slug and company

Greenfly⎤
Slug   ⎬   Down with the Big Ones!
Maggot⎦   Up, Resistance Underground!
                          Down with the Big Ones!
                          Down, down, down.
                          Teach them a lesson!
                          Make their garden look a sight!
                          Down with the Big Ones—
                          Fight, fight, fight.

Red Admiral Glow Worm! What are you doing on their side?

Glow Worm I beg your pardon? I was just on my way home. (*He yawns*)

Slug Take no notice of him and listen to me.

Music for tension sounds underneath the dialogue

   I propose that, until the Big Ones stop using their vile spray, every insect should go on strike, let the garden go to seed, and eat every plant and vegetable in sight.

Greenfly⎤
Maggot ⎬Hear, hear; hooray, etc., etc.

Glow Worm (*realizing*) Oh no! I couldn't possibly agree to that; the Big Ones have always treated me most respectfully.

   (*He sings*)   The Big Ones like me—
                          I keep watch, letting them sleep calm;
                          And ev'ry night
                          My shining light
                          Keeps them from harm.

Maggot "blows out" Glow Worm's lantern

The following section of the song is sung in counterpoint, A and B fitting together with an optional repeat in which Ladybird sings a harmonising coloratura part.

Slug   ⎤
Greenfly⎬   Down with the Big Ones, etc.   A
Maggot ⎦

Glow Worm ⎫		
Bumble Bee ⎬	The Big Ones like me, etc.	B
Red Admiral ⎱		
Ladybird ⎰	*(each singing their own version)*	

As the song ends, Red Admiral comes forward. Red Admiral blows his whistle.

Red Admiral Well then, we must take the vote. Those in favour of fighting the Big Ones by destroying this beautiful garden, whether by going on strike or by eating as many plants and vegetables as possible indicate now.

Slug, Maggot and Greenfly do so

One, two, three. Those against?

Red Admiral, Ladybird, Glow Worm and Bumble Bee vote

One, two, three, four (*With relief*) Then I am pleased to say that, by four votes to three, things are to stay as they are.

Slug and his company react angrily. The others are pleased

Ant enters, with his wheelbarrow empty

Slug Wait a minute. Ant hasn't voted yet. (*He stops Ant*) Ant.
Ant What is it? I really haven't time to stop and chatter.
Greenfly Down with the Big Ones. Do you agree?
Ant I don't really know. Oh dear!
Ladybird Join us, Ant. The Big Ones never do you any harm.
Ant That's true, very true—yes, I'll . . .
Slug What about the time they sprayed the Ant Hill? Sssss. Sssss.
Ant Well, of course, that wasn't very pleasant.
Greenfly Exactly.
Ant But I always thought it was a mistake.
Red Admiral Of course it was.
Slug A mistake?
Bumble Bee They didn't mean it.
Greenfly The Big Ones never make mistakes.
Glow Worm They are only human.
Maggot Down with the Big Ones!
Ant Oh dear, what shall I do, (*To the Audience*) What do you think I should do? What shall I vote for? Down with the Big Ones?

The Audience reaction is led by Slug and company

Or Up with the Big Ones?

The Audience reaction is led by Red Admiral and company. This continues to and fro as necessary

Oh I don't know . . .

The Red Admiral blows his whistle for silence

I did have to spend a week in the Insect Hospital having all that spray removed . . . All right—*Down with the Big Ones.*

Ant joins Slug and company, and they rejoice. The others look very downcast

Now I must get on. All this wasting time, hurry scurry, hurry scurry.

Ant exits with his wheelbarrow

Slug So it's four all—a draw. What do you say to that, Admiral?
Red Admiral All I can say is, as there is a draw, four votes all, we must all do as we feel is right, and hope that our ship will not sink in the process. (*He takes the map and steps to the cocoon*)

Glow Worm, Bumble Bee and Ladybird follow

I declare the meeting closed. Come, shipmates, back to my cabin.

Red Admiral exits to the cocoon, where he hangs up the map. His company follow

Greenfly You haven't heard the last of us.
Maggot Down with the Big Ones!
Slug We'll fight. We'll destroy the garden. We'll stop you working and looking pretty and giving the Big Ones pleasure.
Maggot Down with the Big Ones!
Greenfly Be quiet.
Slug No. Why should he be? He's right. DOWN WITH THE BIG ONES!

SONG: DOWN WITH THE BIG ONES! (reprise) 5a

Slug ⎫	Down with the Big Ones!
Greenfly ⎬	Up Resistance Underground!
Maggot ⎭	Down with the Big Ones—
	Down, down, down.
	Teach them a lesson!
	Make their garden look a sight!
	Down with the Big Ones—
	Fight, fight, fight! 5b

The Lights snap to a Black-out during which Slug, Greenfly and Maggot take off the banners, strike the seats and tables. The Red Admiral opens the cocoon.

Scene 2

The Red Admiral's home—an old cocoon which is decorated to resemble a ship's cabin. Night

As the Lights go up, Glow Worm is seen asleep, Red Admiral looking out of the window through his telescope, Ladybird sitting writing on a barrel

Bumble Bee appears and approaches the cocoon, with his satchel

Red Admiral Here he comes! I think so, anyway.

Bumble Bee knocks on the door

What's the password?

Bumble Bee (*outside*) The ant is anti the antirrhinum.

Red Admiral It's him. (*He opens the door*) Come aboard.

Bumble Bee goes into the cocoon

Make yourself at home.

Ladybird Well, what news?

Bumble Bee I think we are safe for a while. They've been in Slug's cabbage for ages and they can't do much now because it's night time.

Glow Worm (*waking up with a start*) Night time? (*He falls off his chair*) Oh dear, I'm sorry. I've overslept. I'd better fetch my lantern and go to work.

Bumble Bee Not tonight, Glow Worm.

Glow Worm What?

Bumble Bee No work tonight.

Glow Worm Not go to work, But that's impossible. What if something happens to the garden?

Ladybird But worse still, what if something happens to *you*? (*She pats Glow Worm's hand*)

Red Admiral The mood Slug is in, he might try anything.

Glow Worm Then what are we to do?

Red Admiral We shelter here until the storm passes. It may be days, it may be weeks . . .

Glow Worm Oh, I hope not.

There is a pause of general gloom

Ladybird Perhaps I should prepare a little supper for us all.

Red Admiral I'm sorry, Ladybird. I'm right out of rations. The cupboard is bare.

Glow Worm Then it would appear we cannot stay here for days, let alone weeks. A few hours maybe . . .

Bumble Bee I've got some nectar in my sacks, we could share that. I'm sure the Queen Bee wouldn't mind—in the circumstances.

All Thank you, etc.

They each take a handful and enjoy it

Red Admiral (*suddenly*) Shiver me timbers, I've got it!

All jump with surprise

The Great Mushroom.

Glow Worm The great what?

Red Admiral Mushroom!

Glow Worm What about him?

Red Admiral He'll be able to advise us.

Bumble Bee Yes, of course, there's nothing he doesn't know about.

Glow Worm I don't think I recollect the gentleman.

Red Admiral Oh, Glow Worm, you remember when it didn't rain for days and days last summer and we were all so thirsty, the Great Mushroom told us about what the Big Ones call the "dripping tap".

Glow Worm I remember—he saved our lives and he lives on the compost heap.

Red Admiral That's right. (*Looking at the map*) Just here—forty-two sou' sou' west. Let's go.

Ladybird Is it safe?

Bumble Bee If we stick together.

Red Admiral And if I take my compass. (*He picks up a compass from his chest*)

Ladybird That compost heap is rather smelly.

Red Admiral Who cares about that if we can get things shipshape again.

Ladybird All right, let's go!

Glow Worm (*enthusiastically picking up his lantern*) I'll lead the way! To the Great Mushroom! (*He makes to go*)

Ladybird stops Glow Worm with a motion of her hand, and picks up her notebook and pencil

SONG: THE GREAT MUSHROOM   6

All (*singing*)

    Intro:

        He knows all, never goes to sleep,
        He lives high on the compost heap,
        With apple cores, banana skins, potato peel;
        Right under
        The left-overs.
        He can tell us what the future will reveal.

    Chorus:

        We'll ask
        The Great Mushroom
        The Great Mushroom—
        For the Great Mushroom's sure to know
        Just what to do.
        We'll ask
        The Great Mushroom
        The Great Mushroom—
        To the Great Mushroom here we go.
        His home is damp and rotten
        But his words can't be forgotten
        His wisdom good and pure
        Shines forth from the manure.

They start to leave the cocoon,

> We'll ask
> The Great Mushroom
> The Great Mushroom—
> For the Great Mushroom must have some
> Advice to spare.
> We'll ask
> The Great Mushroom
> The Great Mushroom—
> To the Great Mushroom here we come.
> He'll help us out of trouble
> If we find him in the rubble.
> He'll do a magic spell
> If we can stand the smell.

They start moving to the compost heap

Repeat of second chorus

> We'll ask
> The Great Mushroom
> The Great Mushroom—
> For the Great Mushroom isn't far—
> We're nearly there,
> We'll ask
> The Great Mushroom
> The Great Mushroom—
> At the Great Mushroom's here we are.

They arrive at the compost heap

There they find the Great Mushroom, who has been drawn on on his truck

Bumble Bee Here he is. (*He buzzes round in excitement*)
Glow Worm (*shining his lantern*) He's grown considerably since our last visit.
Ladybird It's such an excellent compost heap! Though it *is* a little smelly.

They have all noticed this fact, and react to it

Red Admiral Right now, I think he's asleep. Lower your heads while I wake him up.

They all lower their heads

Good evening, O Great Mushroom.

No reaction from the Great Mushroom. Red Admiral and Ladybird peer round

Glow Worm Do you think he's all right?
Bumble Bee Must be a bit deaf, I think.
Glow Worm Pardon?
Bumble Bee *A bit deaf!!*

Glow Worm Perhaps I am. It's the cold air, you know.
Bumble Bee Not you—the *Mushroom*!
Glow Worm What about him?
Bumble Bee Never mind.
Red Admiral (*to Ladybird*) Perhaps we should *all* say good evening.
Ladybird Good idea. Perhaps we should *shout* it.
Red Admiral Tophole. Shout it, yes. One, two, three.
All but Glow Worm Good evening O Great Mushroom.

Glow Worm, realizing half-way through what is happening, joins in a few words behind the others. No reaction

Ladybird Oh dear.
Bumble Bee Perhaps if everybody—(*taking in the Audience*)—shouted, he might hear?
Glow Worm He might what?
Bumble Bee Hear!
Glow Worm Hear, hear!
Red Admiral Good wheeze. Let's have a practice. After I say "One, two, three", everybody shout.

They direct a rehearsal. Eventually—

All One, two, three.
Audience Good evening, O Great Mushroom.

The four stand in a huddle in front of the Great Mushroom conducting the Audience. They do not see him begin to move forward, perhaps with lights flashing. The Audience shout out that he is coming and the four congratulate themselves on how well they can shout. Meanwhile—perhaps over a loud-speaker—we hear strange noises from the Mushroom as he advances. In fact, he is building up to an enormous sneeze. When this comes, the four jump, and react to his being awake. Great Mushroom produces a large handkerchief and uses it. He has a cold. All four prostrate themselves

All Ah! Great Mushroom, Great Mushroom, etc.
Great Mushroom Get up, get up—a—

They start to rise

—tishoo!

The four fall down again. This is repeated if necessary

What can I do for you? Don't get too near, I've got a filthy cold. It's so draughty here at this time of year.
Glow Worm Yes, indeed; at night there is quite a breeze.
Great Mushroom You're telling me!
Glow Worm You need a good mustard bath for your stalk.
Red Admiral Great Mushroom, we know you know everything—
Bumble Bee—and we know that you know that we know you know every-thing—
Ladybird—so . . .

Great Mushroom Wait, wait. I'm lost already.
Red Admiral (*starting again*) You know everything.
Great Mushroom Yes.
Ladybird So we've come to ask your advice.
Bumble Bee You see, Slug, Greenfly and Maggot are plotting.
Great Mushroom I know.
Red Admiral You know?
Great Mushroom You've just said I know everything.
Red Admiral Of course!
Great Mushroom Would you like to see them and hear what they are plotting?
All Yes, please.
Glow Worm But it's rather a long journey.
Red Admiral And we've only just arrived.
Bumble Bee I think the Great Mushroom means by magic.
Red Admiral Oh! Yes, please.
Great Mushroom Such a privilege must be worth something. What will you give me?
Red Admiral (*realizing*) Oh! Of course. (*Seeing Ladybird's notebook and pencil, he grabs them*) Here you are.
Ladybird Oh!
Great Mushroom What's this?
Ladybird (*a little upset*) My notebook and pencil.
Great Mushroom What can I do with these?
Red Admiral (*stumped*) Er . . .
Bumble Bee Write your memoirs.
Red Admiral Exactly. The Memoirs of the Great Mushroom.
Great Mushroom Well . . .
Glow Worm I would certainly buy a copy—perhaps two—my cousin would be most interested.
Great Mushroom Oh, all right.

They give him the notebook and pencil

Now look straight ahead

The four look straight ahead, Red Admiral using his telescope

—and wiggle your tentacles, antennae or fingers; or whatever you have, wiggle them. Watch and wiggle. Watch—

The Audience is encouraged to do this too

—and wiggle.

The Lights cross-fade to the inside of Slug's cabbage. Slug, Maggot and Greenfly are inside, with Maggot eating as usual and making a loud noise, as he sits on a box

Slug So, the more nasty and horrible we can make the garden, the better!
Greenfly Make it really nasty for the Big Ones.

Maggot (*bouncing on his box*) Down with the Big Ones!

Slug }
Greenfly } Be quiet

Greenfly And don't talk with your mouth full.

Maggot (*speaking through a full mouth*) I wasn't tttalking with my mmmouth fffull, was I, Uncle Slug?

Greenfly Don't argue. (*She clouts Maggot*)

Slug Please can we get on? Tomorrow morning we will stop Bumble Bee working—this way none of the plants will be pollinated, so there won't be any pretty flowers for the Big Ones to look at. He! He! He!

All laugh

Maggot Can I do that?

Greenfly What?

Maggot Stop Bumble Bee working.

Greenfly Ask your Uncle Slug.

Maggot (*bouncing on his box*) Can I, Uncle Slug?

Slug We'll see—if you're *Very* good.

Maggot puts on a "good" expression

Now then, there is Ladybird.

Greenfly Let me deal with her. I'll lie in wait for her and catch her, and then she won't be able to land on the Big Ones' hands and they won't have any good luck. He! He! He!

All laugh

Slug Then there's the Admiral. Leave him to me. I'll teach him. Just because he's all in pretty colours the Big Ones like him. I'll catch him and they'll never see him again.

Maggot What about Glow Worm?

Greenfly We must stop him from working too.

Slug That can wait until tomorrow night. He'll be asleep all day. But by tomorrow midnight our plan will be well on the way to success!

Maggot Down with the Big Ones!

All Down with the Big Ones!

SONG: DOWN WITH THE BIG ONES! (Reprise)   7

(*Singing*)   Down with the Big Ones!
Up Resistance Underground!
Down with the Big Ones
Down, down, down.
Teach them a lesson!
Make their garden look a sight!
Down with the Big Ones
Fight, fight, fight.

The Lights cross-fade back to the compost heap

Great Mushroom Atishoo!

The four turn and listen

If you listen, I will help you.
All Thank you, etc., etc. It's very kind of him, isn't it, etc.

They wait eagerly

Great Mushroom Surely my advice is worth something? What will you give me?
Red Admiral Oh dear! What have we got?
Bumble Bee What about your telescope?
Red Admiral Oh! I don't think the Great Mushroom would want that. (*He hides his telescope*)
Ladybird Or your compass, Admiral.
Red Admiral We need that to find our way back to port. (*He hides his compass*)
Glow Worm Have we something for the poor vegetable's cold?
Bumble Bee Well, there's a little nectar left—might be good for a sore throat.
Red Admiral Excellent wheeze. Give him some of that.
Bumble Bee Here we are, O Great Mushroom. (*He opens his satchel and holds it out*) For your throat.
Great Mushroom Ah! Thank you, most kind. (*He takes some nectar and rubs it on his throat*)
Bumble Bee Er—you're meant to eat it, O Great Mushroom.
Great Mushroom Oh, very well. (*He swallows the nectar*) Now, the life of the garden must not be allowed to come to a standstill. The garden must not die.
All Hear, hear. Quite right, etc., etc.
Great Mushroom Sssh.

All are quiet

If ever Slug, Greenfly or Maggot try to catch you or stop you working in the garden, you are to make noises which sound like the Big Ones. This will make Slug, Greenfly and Maggot run to hide for fear of being sprayed, and you will be able to escape. (*He sneezes*)
All That's marvellous. Brilliant idea, etc., etc.
Ladybird But what "noises" should we make?
Great Mushroom You should make noises as follows: (*In a low man's voice*) "Come along, darling, let's have a look at the garden." (*In a woman's high voice*) "All right, dear, but don't get your feet muddy." (*He hisses*) Sssssss!
Glow Worm What does Sssssss mean, exactly?
Great Mushroom That's the noise of the spray. (*He sniffs*) Now you'll have to excuse me. I must go and try your mustard bath.
Glow Worm Yes. Please do—it will do you the world of good.
Great Mushroom I hope so. Good night.

All Bye bye, etc. etc.

The four bow their heads

The Great Mushroom is drawn off on his truck

Glow Worm What a charming vegetable!

Red Admiral What a brilliant wheeze—make noises like the Big Ones!

Ladybird But there is a problem.

Bumble Bee What?

Ladybird Well, we have to make a high noise and a low noise. I don't think I'll be very good at the low one. I wouldn't fool Slug and his friends. They would soon find out I wasn't the Big Ones.

Bumble Bee She's right, I can't do that sort of thing either. I can do (*in a low voice*) "Come on darling, let's have a look at the garden" but I'm not very good at (*trying a high voice*) "All right dear, but don't get your feet muddy".

Ladybird (*trying a low voice*) "Come on darling, let's have a look at . . ." No, it's no use.

Red Admiral (*trying a high voice*) "All right, dear, but don't get your feet muddy." Yes, I see the problem.

Glow Worm Excuse me, Admiral. I have an idea. Perhaps if everybody (*taking in the Audience*) could do it, it might sound better.

Red Admiral How do you mean?

Glow Worm Well, if all the boys and gentlemen say "Come on, darling, let's have a look at the garden" as low as they can, and all the girls and ladies say "All right, dear, but don't get your feet muddy" as high as they can, and then if they could *all* make a hissing noise for the spray . . .

Red Admiral Excellent plan. Right, let's get organized. Bumble Bee, you take charge of the boys, Ladybird, look after the girls, and you, Glow Worm, supervise the Sssssss's. And I'll blow my whistle.

Each section is rehearsed in turn, using Red Admiral's whistle to give the children their cue.

Bumble Bee As soon as you hear the whistle, all the boys and gents say as low as they can "Come on, darling, let's have a look at the garden" . . . One, two, three—whistle!

Red Admiral blows the whistle

The low voices practise

Ladybird Now, when they've said that, all the little girls and ladies say as high as they can "All right, dear, but don't get your feet muddy." . . .

The high voices practise

Glow Worm And then everybody go Sssssss . . .

Everyone hisses. This is done several times

Red Admiral Now we're going to put all these things together, one after the other, starting when you hear the whistle, after one, two, three. One, two, three.

Red Admiral blows the whistle

Everyone practises

Now, I'm going to put the whistle over here—(*hanging the whistle on a hook*)—and I'm going to be Slug, so when you hear the whistle, you all do what we've just practised.

Red Admiral exits downstage, re-enters upstage, goes to the whistle and blows

(*After the Audience has participated*) Now it's going to have to be much louder than that.

Red Admiral goes off again, returns, and blows the whistle as before

(*Eventually*) Tophole. Now don't forget. If you see something suspicious, let us know and we'll blow the whistle and then we'll all do the Big Ones' noises.

Bumble Bee Ooo! I can't wait.

SONG: LET OUR GARDEN GROW   8

All   Let our garden grow
                                Is our urgent cry,
                                Let our garden grow,
                                Don't let it fade and die.
                                It's such a peaceful place
                                We've been so happy here,
                                It would be tragic
                                Should the magic
                                Disappear.
                                Let our garden grow
                                Is our urgent cry,
                                Let our garden grow
                                Don't let it fade and die.
                                Let the breezes blow,
                                Let the waterfall flow—
                                But most of all
                                Let our garden grow.

The Lights fade to a Black-out

SCENE 3   9

The garden as in Scene One

Music is heard as dawn breaks the next day. Glow Worm knocks up Ladybird and gives her her paper as before. She returns indoors. He then knocks up Ant, who, as in Scene One, scampers off with his wheelbarrow. Bumble Bee enters with his ladder. He waves to Glow Worm. Glow Worm exits, yawning. Bumble Bee puts his ladder against a flower and collects pollen. He then goes to a second flower, places the ladder against it, turns and faces front to check that his bags are straight. Maggot surreptitiously emerges from Slug's cabbage and nips behind a flower before creeping out, taking the ladder and putting it against another flower. Bumble Bee goes to climb the ladder, but of course finds it is not there. He is soon told by the Audience that it is against the other flower. As he thanks them, Maggot re-emerges and moves the ladder again. The business is repeated. Bumble Bee asks who is doing it

Audience Maggot!
Bumble Bee Who?
Audience *Maggot!*
Bumble Bee Oh! (*He goes to the whistle and waits*)

Maggot enters

Bumble Bee blows the whistle. Audience participation

Maggot exits terrified. Bumble Bee quietly goes up the flower, collects the pollen and exits, thanking the Audience.

The music continues

Greenfly enters. She looks off and sees Ladybird approaching

Greenfly Here comes Ladybird. I'll trip her up and catch her. (*She pulls a long leaf or blade of grass down to near ground level, intending to trip up Ladybird, then hides gleefully*)

Ladybird enters and walks forward towards the trap

The Audience tell her to be careful. She stops in the nick of time to ask the audience what is the matter. The Audience reply that Greenfly is there. Ladybird goes to the whistle and waits. Greenfly wonders why Ladybird hasn't arrived and comes out to look

Greenfly Where is she?

Ladybird blows the whistle. Audience participation. Greenfly starts to run off, but trips over her own trap! She exits

Ladybird thanks the Audience, and exits

The Music continues as Slug emerges from his cabbage

Slug (*to the Audience*) You slimy goody-goodies; I've been watching from my cabbage, and the Big Ones haven't come out at all! It's *you* making silly noises. Grrrh! But you can't make it work again; this time it's our turn to laugh. (*Calling off*) Greenfly! Maggot! (*To the Audience*) You just watch this.

Greenfly and Maggot enter, struggling with a huge flowerpot

We'll catch Red Admiral in this flowerpot. He'll be here any minute.

Greenfly and Maggot hold the pot ready to be dropped over someone

(*To the Audience*) Now look here, you slimies, don't you dare tell him we're here. You keep those little mouths *shut*, do you understand? (*He looks off*) Here he comes! (*He rejoins the others*)

Red Admiral enters from his cocoon

The flowerpot follows him. The Audience warn him, but he pretends not to understand. The flowerpot creeps slowly nearer and nearer—wherever he goes it follows him. Finally, in the nick of time, the Lights fade and the noises of the real Big Ones are heard. A door slams

Man (*off*) Come along, darling, let's have a look at the garden.
Woman (*off*) All right, dear, but don't get your feet muddy.

Red Admiral turns, sees Slug and company, and exits quickly

The spray starts. Slug and company drop the flowerpot on its side and run around terrified, eventually running inside the pot to take shelter

Red Admiral enters again and beckons to Ladybird and Bumble Bee who enter quickly and overturn the flowerpot onto Slug and company

The spraying stops and the Lights return to normal. We hear the back door slam

Red Admiral Well done, everyone!

SONG: LET OUR GARDEN GROW (reprise)   9a

All   Let the breezes blow,
                Let the waterfalls flow—
                But most of all
                Let our garden grow.

Ladybird, Red Admiral and Bumble Bee exit

The Lights fade to a Black-out

SCENE 4

Inside the flowerpot

Slug, Maggot and Greenfly are seen crouching inside the pot, perhaps behind a gauze. Maggot and Greenfly are crying loudly

Slug Escape, escape, (*He pushes against the wall—no reaction*) There *must* be a way out.

Silence

Maggot I'm hungry. (*He stands*)
Greenfly Sssh! (*He pushes Maggot down*)
Slug Got it!
Greenfly (*excitedly*) What?
Slug Spider! Spider can help us, we go to see Spider and . . .
Greenfly But how can we go and see Spider when we're stuck in here?
Slug Damnation. You're right.
Maggot I'm going out to get something to eat. (*He stands*)
Greenfly All right, dear, don't be long.
Maggot I won't. Bye, bye.
Slug (*realizing*) Going out? How?
Maggot Through that little hole up there. (*He indicates the hole in the "bottom" of the flowerpot which is above them*)
Slug Don't be so ridic . . . the boy's right! That hole—we're too big to get through it, but he may be able to.
Maggot Help me up, Uncle Slug.

Slug and Greenfly take hold of maggot

Greenfly Be careful with him, he's only a baby.
Slug Ready. One, two, three, heave.

They lift Maggot and then fall under him

Try again.

One two, three, heave. On me shoulders.

This time Maggot gets his head and arms through the hole

He's there! Now push up.
Maggot I cccan't. I'm ssstuck!
Greenfly Then come down again.
Maggot I cccan't ggget dddown either. (*He starts to cry*)

Ant enters the garden with his wheelbarrow, quietly muttering to himself

Ant (*as he crosses the garden*) No time to waste. Hurry scurry, hurry scurry.

Ant has nearly gone off the other side when Maggot sees him

Maggot *Ant!*

Ant stops

Ant Morning, Maggot. What silly game are you playing today? Can't stop. (*He starts to go*)
Maggot Ant! Ppplease. I'm stuck.

Ant Oh! Very well. (*He returns to the pot*) Take this. (*He throws up a rope from his wheelbarrow*) Now pull yourself out.

Ant holds the rope as Maggot lifts himself out onto the top of the flowerpot

Greenfly Are you all right, dear?
Ant (*looking all round*) Who was that?
Maggot My mother. (*He looks down the hole*) Yes, Mummy. Ant hhhelped me.
Slug Maggot.
Maggot Yes, Uncle Slug?
Slug Tell Ant he is to stop working, to go on strike immediately and to go with you to see Spider.
Maggot Yes, Uncle. (*To Ant*) Uncle Slug says you're to go on strike and cccome with me to see Ssspider.
Ant What for?
Maggot (*down the hole*) Wwwhat for?
Slug To get the stickiest web she has. The Admiral and the others are bound to come back here to discuss peace—and we'll be ready for them with a sticky web. Ha! Ha!
Maggot All right. (*To Ant*) We've got to ask her for a web.
Ant What for?
Maggot To catch the Admiral and his crew.
Ant Come on, then.
Maggot But how do I get down?
Ant Put the rope through the hole and ask your Uncle to hang on to it.
Maggot Hang on to this, Uncle. (*He throws the rope down, if possible hitting Slug*)

Slug holds the rope

Ant Now climb down.
Slug (*calling*) Maggot!
Maggot Yes, Uncle Slug?
Slug Be careful not to say why you want the web—Spider might not let you have it if you do.
Maggot I'll remember.

Music is heard as Maggot climbs down the flowerpot on the rope like a mountaineer. When he gets there Ant gives a tug on the rope and Slug releases it. Ant winds it up and puts it back on the wheelbarrow   10

Ant Ready?
Maggot Ready. (*Calling*) Spider! Spider!

Ant and Maggot go (if possible) down into the auditorium through the Audience, asking if anyone has seen Spider, and exit through the back doors. Ant takes his barrow

The Lights fade to a Black-out

SCENE 5

Spider's home—possibly a hole in a stone

Spider is discovered sitting at her spinning wheel, and there are webs hanging up to dry and decorating the "room". Ant and Maggot enter through the door at the front of the auditorium, again asking the Audience whether they have seen Spider. Told by the Audience where she is, they reach the stage and talk out of her hearing

Ant Now don't forget what Slug told you.
Maggot No (*After a pause*) Whwhwhat did he tell me?
Ant You silly boy. He said don't tell Spider what we want the web for.
Maggot Wwwhy not?
Ant Well, I suppose because she's a friend of the Admiral and Ladybird and Bumble Bee.
Maggot Oh! Right!
Ant I'd better do the talking.

They approach Spider gingerly. When they get near Ant opens his mouth to speak, but Spider takes them by surprise by speaking first very sharply

Spider Good day!

Ant drops his barrow

Maggot Hello, Spider
Spider (*sharply again*) What do you two want?

Ant and Maggot jump and tremble at the knees

Ant We want a web, please.
Spider What for?
Maggot To catch Ad . . .

Ant stamps on his foot or slaps him

Maggot Ow!
Ant Sssh!
Spider What did you say?
Maggot Ow—

Ant nudges him

  —are you keeping, Spider?
Spider Stop playing the fool, you stupid boy. (*Fiercely*) Tell me the truth—what are you going to do with one of my webs?
Maggot (*terrified*) We're going to catch Ad . . .
Ant (*stamping on him again*) Sssssshhh!

Maggot starts to cry

Spider Stop crying, you stupid boy. Going to catch what?
Ant (*good at improvising*) Going to catch cold, Spider—in the winter—unless we have an extra web to keep us warm—please.
Maggot (*recovering*) Yes, *please*.

Spider Very well, then. What can I have in exchange?
Ant Anything from my wheelbarrow. (*He takes the barrow near Spider and retreats immediately*)
Spider Thanks. I'll take that rope, it could be useful.
Ant All right. (*He gives Spider the rope*) Now, can we take this one? (*He goes to a web that is hanging up*)
Spider Be careful, it's not dry yet—it's very, very sticky.

Maggot and Ant look at each other gleefully

If anyone were to touch it they would stick to it for ever!
Maggot Oh! Good.
Spider What do you mean, good?
Maggot Good—gracious. When will it be dry?
Spider Not for several days and nights.
Maggot Come on, Ant, let's take it. (*He goes to the web*)
Spider Don't *touch* it. Wear these. (*She gives them each a pair of gloves*) They are anti-web-stick gloves.

Ant and Maggot put on the gloves

Roll the web up carefully and put it on your wheelbarrow. I'd better spray the barrow with this special anti-web-stick spray.

Spider sprays the barrow from a pair of bellows

Ant Thank you, Spider.
Spider And be careful!

Music plays as Ant and Maggot fold up the web and put it on the wheelbarrow **10a**

Ant and Maggot exit through the auditorium with the barrow, and Spider exits to her home

The Lights fade to a Black-out

SCENE 6

Red Admiral's home

The cocoon opens as the Lights come up. Glow Worm is sitting in the chair, very tired, his lantern by him. Red Admiral, Ladybird and Bumble Bee are telling him what has happened. The map is on the wall, and a bugle nearby

Bumble Bee And so they went to hide in the flowerpot.
Red Admiral And I tipped it over on top of them.
Glow Worm I hope there wasn't a flower in it?
Bumble Bee No. Actually—(*turning towards Red Admiral*)—we *all* turned it over
Red Admiral Ah! Yes, but I actually planned the operation.
Ladybird Yes, you were very brave, Admiral.
Red Admiral Well, it's the training, you know. I remember the campaign in forty-three. I was in command of . . .

Glow Worm snores

Glow Worm!

Glow Worm wakes up with a start

I'm talking.

Glow Worm I'm so sorry, I'm a little tired.

Red Admiral I called the crew on deck. They lined up, brave and true, the lot of them, they knew this might be the—

Glow Worm is nodding off again

—last day of their nobly given lives. "Men", I said . . .

Glow Worm It's no use. I shall have to go to bed.

Red Admiral It's no use. I shall have to go to bed. No! I didn't say that. *Glow Worm!*

The music of the song starts   **11**

Glow Worm Forgive me, Admiral. I've been on night shift and now it's morning. I'm so s-l-e-e-p-y- . . .

SONG: IT'S AN UPSIDE DOWN WORLD

Glow Worm (*singing*)

> For a Glow Worm
> On the go worm
> Life's ever so hard:
> Hardly sleeping,
> Ever keeping
> A watch on the gard-
> -en; while most insects play
> I'm shining my light
> For they work all day
> And I work all night.
>
> It's an upside down world.
> It's an upside down world.
> It's an inside out
> Back to front
> Wrong way round world.
>
> For a Glow Worm
> On the go worm
> Life's ever so tough.
> Please excuse me—
> Don't accuse me—
> Don't get in a huff,
> Adm'ral—I try so hard (*He falls against the*
>   *Admiral*)

The Admiral pushes Glow Worm upright again

> An int'rest to take—
> But once off my guard
> I can't keep awake. (*He bends over, laying his
> head on the chair*)

All   It's an upside down world etc.

Glow Worm (*getting slower and slower*) It's an upside down world etc.

Glow Worm falls asleep, sinking from his chair to the floor

Ladybird Let's leave him to sleep.

Red Admiral But what about my story?

Ladybird Another time, Admiral.

Bumble Bee Anyway, I think we ought to discuss what we do next with Slug and Co.

Red Admiral Of course. (*He goes to his map*) Now, we are positioned here; the enemy are under a flowerpot estimated position thirty-three latitude forty-eight longitude here, in a line due east of the cabbage patch. Now, supposing we advance to here, take them by surprise and . . .

Bumble Bee Admiral.

Red Admiral Yes?

Bumble Bee Why don't we just talk to them?

Red Admiral Talk to them?

Ladybird Yes! Talk to them. They must be hungry by now. I'm sure they'll agree to behave better.

Red Admiral Perhaps you're right. A peace treaty. We agree to let them out if they stop their ridiculous plan to beat the Big Ones by catching us or stopping us working. (*He takes his bugle*)

Bumble Bee Exactly. Come on, let's go now.

Ladybird What about poor Glow Worm?

Red Admiral Leave him here. He wouldn't be much help in an emergency, always nodding off; and it's daytime now, we can see without his lantern.

Bumble Bee Come on, then. To the flowerpot!

Red Admiral blows his bugle   11a

Red Admiral, Bumble Bee and Ladybird exit, almost marching

The Lights fade to a Black-out. The cocoon closes. Slug and Greenfly push the flowerpot into position

SCENE 7

The flowerpot

Ant and Maggot, calling "Mum", "Uncle Slug" etc., enter with the web in the wheelbarrow, if possible through the auditorium. As they arrive at the flowerpot the Lights change so that the interior is visible once more

Maggot (*knocking on the flowerpot*) Mum—Uncle Slug!
Slug Did you see Spider?
Maggot Yes, Uncle Slug,
Slug Have you got the web?
Maggot Yes, Uncle Slug.
Slug Is it very, very sticky?
Maggot Yes, Uncle Slug.
Slug Stop saying "Yes, Uncle Slug".
Maggot Yes, Uncle Slug.
Slug (*sharply*) Ant!
Ant Yes, Uncle Slug . . . Yes?
Slug You and Maggot carefully prepare the web and stand where you can throw it over Admiral and Co.

They start to unload

Greenfly And be careful! Look after my little boy, Ant.
Ant Yes, Greenfly. Come on, Maggot. Hurry scurry, hurry scurry.
Slug Are you ready?
Maggot Nearly, Uncle Slug.

They get into position ready. We hear Red Admiral's bugle off

Slug Quick! Here they come.

Maggot and Ant finish just in time, and hide behind the cocoon

Red Admiral, Ladybird and Bumble Bee enter. They "march" towards the flowerpot, but stop some way from it so that they are nowhere near the web

Red Admiral Slug! Are you ready to talk terms?
Slug (*laying it on with a sad voice*) Yes, yes—anything, anything. (*He nudges Greenfly*)
Greenfly Anything.
Slug Only let us out of this horrible flowerpot.
Greenfly For my son's sake, if no-one else's, have mercy.

Maggot and Ant become visible from behind the cocoon. Maggot is very concerned because he cannot get the web over them in their present position

Red Admiral I will ask my colleagues what they think.

Red Admiral, Ladybird and Bumble Bee go into a huddle

Slug (*aside*) They sound a long way away.
Greenfly (*aside*) Maggot and Ant won't be able to catch them unless they come nearer.
Red Admiral (*breaking the huddle*) We have decided to let you out.
Slug (*acting again*) Thank you, thank you.
Red Admiral If, and only if, you give up your plan against the Big Ones.
Slug Sorry, I didn't hear that, Admiral.

Red Admiral (*louder*) I said if, and only if, you give up your plan against the
Big Ones.
Slug I still can't hear. You'll have to come nearer.
Red Admiral (*to Ladybird and Bumble Bee*) Shall we? (*He turns to the* **11b**
Audience for confirmation)

*The three of them move towards the flowerpot, and the Audience goes mad
telling them not to go any closer. They carry on, regardless. Eventually they
are all by the flowerpot. The next few lines may not be heard, but if mimed the
idea will be understood*

If you give up your plan against the Big Ones.
Slug Yes, yes.
Greenfly Anything to be free.
Red Admiral Very well, then. (*He puts his bugle in the barrow*)

*Red Admiral, Ladybird and Bumble Bee lift up the flowerpot. Slug and com-
pany rush out. Slug gives the word "Now!", and the web falls and covers
Admiral and company, who struggle unsuccessfully in the "sticky" net*

Slug Ha! Ha! Ha! Got 'em!

Ant, Maggot and Greenfly join him

Maggot Down with the Big Ones!
Slug We'll destroy the garden.
Greenfly Eat all the plants.
Ant Stop working!
Maggot Down with the Big Ones!
Slug Teach them a lesson.
Greenfly They'll never dare spray us again!
Maggot Down with the Big Ones!

SONG: THE PLOTTERS OF CABBAGE PATCH CORNER   **12**

Ant   Strike!
Slug   Eat!
Greenfly Destroy!

All
(*including Maggot*)
                    We are the Plotters of Cabbage Patch Corner
                    We are the Rotters of Cabbage Patch Corner.
                    If you're on your way home
                    In the middle of the night
                    We'll creep up behind you
                    And give you a fright!

Ant and Maggot "scare" Greenfly and Slug

	We're ugly, we're horrible
	We're rough.
Maggot	We're rough.

All	We're creepy, we're crawly,
	We're tough,
Maggot	We're tough.

All	We are the Plotters of Cabbage Patch Corner
	We are the Rotters of Cabbage Patch Corner.
	If you pick up a stone
	We'll be waiting underneath.
Slug	I'd give you a bite if
	I had any teeth.
	We're wicked, we're dangerous,
	We're rough,
Maggot	We're rough.
All	We're creepy, we're crawly,
	We're tough,
Maggot	We're tough.

All	We mean bus'ness
	Everybody knows.
Slug	I'm the boss round here
Others	What he says goes.

All	We are the Plotters of Cabbage Patch Corner
	We are the Rotters of Cabbage Patch Corner,
	And we'll mess up the garden, devour ev'ry plant,
	And catch ev'ry insect

They drag the captives to the middle of the stage

	Who says that we can't?
	We're vicious, we're savage and
	We're rough,
Maggot	We're rough.
All	We're creepy, we're crawly,
	We're tough,
Maggot	We're tough,
All	We are the Plotters, we are the Plotters
	The filthy dirty Rotters
Slug	Of Cabbage Patch Corner.

As the song ends, Greenfly rips a petal off a flower. The four insects begin to devour and destroy the garden as—

the CURTAIN falls

ACT II

Scene 1

The garden as in Act One Scene One, but ravaged! Night

The cocoon, showing Glow Worm asleep, is open, but the light is concentrated on the flowerpot on it's side, in which Red Admiral, Ladybird and Bumble Bee are imprisoned with the sticky web over the front

SONG: ONLY YESTERDAY

Red Admiral	Only yesterday
Ladybird	Ev'rything seemed fine; *(Singing together)*
Bumble Bee	It seemed the sun would always shine.
Bumble Bee	Only yesterday I climbed my ladder
Ladybird	Only yesterday I brushed my spots
Red Admiral	Only yesterday I blew my whistle—
All	Now we're stuck inside a flowerpot.
Red Admiral	I've been in tight corners from Malta to Gibraltar
	But never so close to home.
Bumble Bee	We're hungry, but there's no more honey—
	It's not funny.
Ladybird	Has anybody got a comb?
All	Only yesterday
	We thought we'd won through,
	When Mushroom told us what to do.
Ladybird	Only yesterday I took the minutes
Bumble Bee (*ironically*)	
	Only yesterday we saw the spray—
Red Admiral (*to his pipe; sadly*)	
	Only yesterday I had some baccy—
All	If only yesterday could be today.

Red Admiral I'm hungry.

Ladybird So am I.

Red Admiral Any nectar left, Bumble?

Bumble Bee 'Fraid not, Admiral. The Great Mushroom had the last drop.

Red Admiral So he did.

Ladybird I'm beginning to fear we shall never see your house again, Admiral.

Red Admiral Cheer up, Ladybird. Stiff upper lip and all that.

Ladybird But we'll never get out; nobody even knows we're here.

Bumble Bee If only that hole were bigger; we're all too big to get out of it.

They are all sad for a moment

13

Of course! I have it!

Red Admiral I think we've all had it, old chap.
Bumble Bee Glow Worm!
Red Admiral Glow Worm too—poor old chap.
Ladybird Never hurt anyone, everybody's friend. Kind, helpful . . .
Bumble Bee He can help now.
Red Admiral How?
Bumble Bee Well, look—it's night-time.
Ladybird Well?
Red Admiral Of course. He'll wake up soon!
Bumble Bee Yes, and where is he?
Ladybird In the Admiral's house.
Bumble Bee Where we were . . .
Red Admiral So, he'll wonder where we've gone—
Ladybird —and come and look for us.
Bumble Bee Exactly!

The three talk excitedly as the Light comes up a little to the Red Admiral's house, where Glow Worm is snoring. The Audience may try to waken him: in any case he falls off his chair and wakens

Glow Worm (*thinking the others are still there*) I do beg your pardon—I nearly went to sleep then. Carry on, Admiral, tell me your story . . . (*Realizing*) He's gone! (*Calling*) Ladybird! Bumble Bee! They've all gone. Where on earth can they be?

This should get the Audience shouting "Flowerpot!"

Where? Oh! My! Did Slug and Co catch them? I must get going immediately.   13a

Music is heard as Glow Worm sets off walking very gingerly and carefully shining his lantern

(*Calling softly*) Admiral, Bumble Bee, Ladybird.

The others hear him coming. Admiral comes to the web and Glow Worm creeps gingerly round to look in the top of the flowerpot through the web—their faces meet at the same time and both jump. Glow Worm drops the lantern

Glow Worm Oh! (*He stoops to pick up the lantern, which is still working*)
Red Admiral (*recovering*) Is that you?
Glow Worm Who?
Red Admiral You.
Glow Worm Yes, it's me.
Red Admiral Who?
Glow Worm Glow Worm.
Red Admiral Whew! That's all right, then. Good show, Glow Worm.
Bumble Bee We're trapped in here.
Ladybird Please help us, Glow Worm.

Glow Worm (*going towards Ladybird, and, therefore, the web*) Oh! Poor
  Ladybird, you too? Of course I'll . . .
Red Admiral Halt!

Glow Worm stops

  Don't come any closer.
Glow Worm Why not?
Bumble Bee That web is very sticky and if you touch it you'll never get free.
Glow Worm I'm sorry. Look, exactly what can I do to assist?
Red Admiral That's a good point.
Bumble Bee I know. Go to the Great Mushroom again.
Red Admiral That's right. He'll put us back on course.
Ladybird And please hurry.
Glow Worm I will. (*He turns and immediately falls over. The lantern crashes
  and goes out*) Oh! No!
Red Admiral What's happened?
Glow Worm My lantern's gone out. I'll never find my way now.
Ladybird Try, Glow Worm, try.
Bumble Bee *Ask* someone the way.
Glow Worm Good idea. All right, leave it to me.

  Glow Worm exits gingerly.

SONG: THE GREAT MUSHROOM (Reprise)   13b

(*Singing*)   I'll ask
        The Great Mushroom
        The Great Mushroom—
        For the Great Mushroom's sure to know
        Just what to do.
        I'll ask
        The Great Mushroom
        The Great Mushroom—
        To the Great Mushroom here I go.   14

SCENE 2

Outside Slug's cabbage. Night

*The Lights cross-fade from the flowerpot to the cabbage, and the cocoon is
closed. Greenfly, Slug and Maggot emerge from the cabbage. Slug is much
fatter than in Act One, and Maggot a bit fatter*

Maggot Wwwhat are we going to tell them, Uncle Slug?
Slug We'll demand their support against the Big Ones.
Greenfly And if they don't give it?
Slug We leave them to starve, to starve and perish in misery.

All laugh nastily

Glow Worm enters with his hand outstretched, holding the unlit lantern, and walking very gingerly

Who's that?

For a moment Slug and company recoil

Maggot It's old Glow Worm.

Greenfly Let's catch him and put him in the flowerpot too.

Slug Wait a minute. His lantern has gone out and he can't see at all without it. Stay here. (*He advances on Glow Worm and accidentally on purpose bumps into him*)

Glow Worm Oh!

Slug (*in an assumed voice*) Oh! I do beg your pardon, sir. I wasn't looking where I was going.

Glow Worm That's all right, guvnor. You gave me quite a scare, though! You see, I think I'm lost.

Slug Perhaps I can help you, sir. Where are you going?

Glow Worm To the compost heap to see the Great Mushroom.

Slug Really? Well, you're some way from the compost heap, but I'm sure (*more loudly*) my young nephew would be pleased to guide you there. I'll fetch him.

Glow Worm Oh! Thank you. I'm most grateful.

Slug returns to Greenfly and Maggot who have been listening at a distance, and speaks to Maggot

(*To Maggot*) Lead him anywhere you like, but bring him back *here* in ten minutes.

Maggot Yes, Uncle Slug.

Slug And don't let him know it's you.

Maggot No, Uncle Slug. (*He goes over to Glow Worm*)

Slug Come on, Greenfly, we've got work to do. Have you seen a toadstool recently?

Greenfly A *toadstool*?

Greenfly and Slug exit

Maggot (*taking Glow Worm's hand; in an assumed voice*) Come along, sir, follow me.

They start to walk

Glow Worm Oh! That's most kind of you. I hope I'm not taking you too far out of your way.

Maggot Not at all, sir, This way. (*He leads him back the same way—up and down in a circle*)

Glow Worm How long will the journey take, do you think?

Maggot Oh, about ten minutes. (*He giggles*)

Glow Worm I feel a little giddy.

Maggot That's because we're going up hill. Not much further, sir.

*Maggot leads Glow Worm off, as the Lights cross-fade to the flowerpot,
with an effect of early dawn*   **14a**

SCENE 3

The flowerpot

*Red Admiral, Bumble Bee and Ladybird are resting inside. Ant enters with his
wheelbarrow as though to start work, but slowly and sadly. He stops near the
flowerpot*

Ant I'm not working today. Slug's orders. We're on strike, he says. Teach
the Big Ones a lesson. Well, I don't mind admitting I'm bored. There's no
more hurry scurry, it's all worry, worry. There's nothing worse than
having nothing to do—especially for an Ant.

SONG: AN ANT WAS BORN TO BE BUSY (HURRY SCURRY)   **15**

(*Singing*)   Always hurry, scurry
                     Always in a flurry—
                     An ant was born to be busy, busy—

(*He punches one hand against the other, hurts himself, shakes the hurt hand*)

                     Always busy working
                     Never, never shirking;
                     An Ant is not an Ant if he's not busy, is he?

(*He leans against a step, his fingers miming the next line*)

                     Bustling up and down a tree trunk,
                     Hardly ever rest,
                     Foraging and scavenging,
                     Scuttling to the nest

                     Always hurry, scurry
                     Always in a flurry—
                     An Ant was born to be busy, busy—
                     Always busy working
                     Never, never shirking;
                     An Ant is not an Ant if he's not busy, is he?

                     Scrub the tunnels of the ant hill,
                     Try to keep them clean,
                     To and fro unearthing food,
                     Take it to the Queen.

(*He turns a cartwheel, ending on his knees*)

                     Always hurry, scurry

Always in a flurry—
An Ant was born to be busy, busy—
Always busy working
Never, never shirking;
An Ant is not an Ant if he's not busy
Busy, busy, busy, busy, busy—is he?
(*He leans backward, and collapses on the floor*)

During the song, the prisoners wake and listen. After a moment Ant starts to exit past the flowerpot

Red Admiral Pssst.

Ant stops, then goes on

Psssst. Ant.

Ant stops again. If the Audience have not already shouted out, Red Admiral calls

Behind you.

Ant Hello, Admiral, what are you doing in there?

Red Admiral You should know that. You helped catch us and now we're trapped.

Ant I'm sorry; only carrying out orders. Got to teach the Big Ones a lesson.

Bumble Bee You don't really believe that, do you?

Ant Slug says . . .

Bumble Bee Slug says! What do *you* say?

Ladybird I must say I'm very surprised at you, Ant. It's not like you at all; you're normally so responsible.

Ant (*a bit rattled*) It's all right for you. You haven't been sprayed by the Big Ones. I had to have treatment in the Insect Hospital last time.

Red Admiral It's no use talking to him any more. He's clearly very happy being on strike.

Ant (*going to his barrow*) I never said that.

Bumble Bee It must be so interesting doing nothing all day!

Ant Well, as a matter of fact, I get rather bored.

Ladybird But, as you said, Admiral, let everyone do what he thinks is right.

Ant Well, I'm not really certain I know what's right any more.

Red Admiral Off you go, Ant. We don't need your help. And if you really never want to work again . . .

Ant Oh! But I *do*.

Bumble Bee Then help us. Change sides while you have the chance.

Red Admiral Join us and you'll be able to work again.

Ladybird Stay with Slug and you'll *never* work again.

Bumble Bee Come on, Ant.

Ant (*to the Audience*) Shall I? etc. (*After receiving their advice*) Very well then, I will. What do I have to do?

Red Admiral First put rescue plans into operation and get us out of here!

Ant Certainly, but I'll need my tools—oh, and those anti-web-stick gloves that Spider gave me. It's quite a tricky job.

Bumble Bee Off you go, then.
Ladybird Thank you, Ant. You won't regret it.
Ant (*moving to exit*) Hurry scurry—how exciting, I'm working again—
hurry scurry. Back in a jiffy.

Ant exits, with his barrow   15a

The Lights cross-fade to Slug's cabbage

SCENE 4

Near Slug's cabbage. The atmosphere is rather sinister

Slug and Greenfly drag on a toadstool resembling the Great Mushroom

Slug (*whispering*) We'll put it here.
Greenfly (*whispering*) Hope it works.
Slug With Glow Worm's bad eyesight and with no lantern it can't fail.
Anyway, a toadstool looks very like a mushroom. Get round the back
and we'll have a practice.
Greenfly All right. (*She goes behind the toadstool*)
Slug Now I'll pretend to be Glow Worm. (*He bows his head*) Good morn-
ing, O Great Mushroom.
Greenfly (*in an assumed voice*) Good morning, O Glow Worm.
Slug No, no, no, not "O Glow Worm". Just "Glow Worm".
Greenfly (*in a normal voice*) But you said, "O Great Mushroom".
Slug But that's different. It's a sign of respect "O Great Mushroom".
Try again. Not "O Glow Worm", just "Glow Worm".
Greenfly Right.
Slug Good morning, O Great Mushroom.
Greenfly Good morning, just Glow Worm.
Slug No, no, no.
Greenfly (*coming from behind the toadstool*) What is it now?
Slug You say . . .
Greenfly (*looking off*) Look out, here they come.
Slug Quick.

*Slug and Greenfly turn and bump into each other. Eventually Greenfly gets
behind and Slug stands beside the toadstool on the side away from where
Glow Worm will be*

Maggot and Glow Worm enter

Slug peeps out and indicates the toadstool to Maggot, who understands

Maggot Here we are, the Great Mushroom.
Glow Worm (*stopping*) Oh! Thank you. (*He puts down his lantern and map,
and bows*) Good morning, O Great Mushroom.
Greenfly Good morning, just Glow Worm.

Slug reacts

Glow Worm You sound much better. Did you try the mustard bath?
Greenfly What custard tart?
Glow Worm I beg your pardon?
Greenfly Why should I have tried a custard tart?
Glow Worm No, a mustard bath—for your cold. Did you try one?

There is a pause, Greenfly pops her head out

Slug (*whispering*) Yes, I did.
Greenfly (*whispering*) What?
Slug Yes, I did.
Greenfly (*to Glow Worm*) Yes, he did.
Slug No—you did.
Greenfly No, *you* did.
Glow Worm No, I didn't.
Greenfly Didn't you?
Glow Worm No. Did you?

There is a pause

Slug (*whispering*) Answer his question.
Greenfly (*whispering*) What?
Slug (*a little louder*) Answer his question.
Greenfly (*to Glow Worm; aloud*) I've got indigestion.
Glow Worm Oh dear, I am sorry. You must try some excellent lozenges I
    use.
Slug (*to Greenfly*) What on earth are you on about?
Greenfly (*to Glow Worm*) What on earth are you on about?
Glow Worm The lozenges that I recommend for . . .
Slug *No!*
Greenfly *NO!*
Slug Shut up!
Greenfly Shut up!
Glow Worm I apologize.
Greenfly Granted.
Slug *No*, you apologize.
Greenfly (*sotto voce*) I'm sorry!
Slug Not to *me*—to *him*.
Greenfly (*to Glow Worm*) I'm sorry.
Slug Now get on with it.
Greenfly Now get on with it.
Glow Worm (*taken aback*) Well—I've come for your advice. Three of my
    friends—that is the three you saw yesterday—are trapped in a flowerpot
    with one of Spider's webs. How can I help them?
Greenfly (*as if carefully learned parrot-fashion*) I will put a spell on you, so
    that you will be able to touch the web without getting stuck. Then you
    can pull it down and let the others out.
Glow Worm That sounds splendid.
Greenfly Outstretch your arms.

Glow Worm stretches out his arms

Wiggle your hands and I will say the magic spell. Istomakas; trumpita-boooooom. You are now under the spell. Go back to the flowerpot and rescue your friends.

Glow Worm (*as if in a trance*) I will, O Great Mushroom. O venerable vegetable. Good day.

Greenfly Good morning, just Glow Worm.

Glow Worm exits

Slug emerges. Greenfly comes out and Maggot joins them

Slug Ha ha ha ha—well done! He thinks magic will stop the web from sticking to him.

Maggot But it won't! Ha ha ha ha!

Greenfly He'll get caught in the web . . .

Slug And then we'll have caught all four of them.

SONG: THE PLOTTERS OF CABBAGE PATCH CORNER (Reprise) 16

All (*with Maggot bashing the toadstool like a drum*)
    (*spoken*) Ha ha ha ha
    (*singing*) We are the Plotters of Cabbage Patch Corner
             We are the Rotters of Cabbage Patch Corner,
             And we'll mess up the garden,
             Devour ev'ry plant
             And catch ev'ry insect—
             Who says that we can't?

Maggot   We're vicious, we're savage, we're rough. We're rough.
All   We're creepy, we're crawly,
               We're tough.
Maggot   We're tough.

Maggot makes an extravagant gesture and thumps Slug in the stomach

All   We are the Plotters, We are the Plotters,
               The filthy dirty Rotters
Maggot & Greenfly ⎱ The Plotters
Slug   ⎰ Of Cabbage Patch Corner

They all exit, Slug carrying the toadstool

Fade to blackout
                                         16a

SCENE 5

The flowerpot. Daytime

Bumble Bee, Ladybird and Red Admiral are inside as before

Red Admiral He must be nearly here. It's daytime.
Bumble Bee Shhhh. There's someone coming.

They watch Glow Worm off stage

Ladybird Oh, it's Glow Worm.
Red Admiral Splendid chap. I knew he'd do it.
Bumble Bee Why is he walking like that? He can't be asleep.
Ladybird He's heading this way.

Glow Worm enters, arms outstretched as if enchanted

Red Admiral Glow Worm!

No reaction

Bumble Bee He's heading straight for the web.
Ladybird He'll be caught . . .
All Stop, stop. Wake up, etc.

In the nick of time, Glow Worm seems to recover consciousness

Glow Worm Good morning.
Red Admiral What are you doing?
Glow Worm (*putting down his lantern and map*) I'm going to get you out.
Bumble Bee But how?
Glow Worm Ah! The Great Mushroom has put a spell on me! I can tear this web down without getting stuck.
Ladybird But that's impossible!
Red Admiral Sounds fishy to me.
Bumble Bee I think it may be a trick. (*To the Audience*) Is it? Did Slug and Co. organize it? There you are, Glow Worm, you're no more enchanted than me.
Glow Worm Oh! What a shame. I really *felt* enchanted. Can't you get out of the little hole at the back?
Red Admiral No, we've tried. We're too big.

Ant enters, very business-like, with two ropes, one with a hook, and gloves in his barrow

Ant Hurry scurry, here we are; excuse me, Glow Worm, no time to lose. (*He nearly knocks Glow Worm over with his barrow*)
Red Admiral Good show, Ant—got all your equipment?
Ant Yes, rope, hooks, gloves . . .
Glow Worm Good gracious, are you going on an expedition?
Ant No, Glow Worm, I'm going to rescue those three poor prisoners. Glad

you're here, you can give me a hand. (*He lays the hooked rope by the barrow and the long rope beside it*)

Ladybird Now do be careful—both of you.

Bumble Bee Glow Worm looks a little tired to me.

Glow Worm I must admit I am a wee bit sleepy. You see, it's morning again and I really should be in bed.

Ant (*giving him one anti-web-stick glove*) Take this and put it on.

Glow Worm What about the other one?

Ant I'm wearing that. (*He puts it on*)

Glow Worm It's not much good having one cold hand and one warm hand.

Ant Maybe not, but at least you have one hand that can touch the web without getting stuck. Now, stand there. (*He places Glow Worm to one side of the flowerpot*)

Glow Worm I wish I didn't feel so sleepy.

Ant collects one of the ropes and stands to the other side of the flowerpot

Ant Catch this. (*He throws one end of the rope over, almost hitting Glow Worm*)

Glow Worm Oh! What's this for?

Ant Well, I have to climb up on the flowerpot, so you hold that rope steady for me.

Glow Worm Very well.

Ant And *don't* fall asleep and drop the rope. It could be very dangerous.

Glow Worm (*yawning*) Very well.

Ant (*to the Audience*) Let me know if he nods off, will you? I don't want to fall off. Here we go.

Ant begins to climb up the flowerpot, and Glow Worm nods off: the Audience participate, shouting to Glow Worm to wake up. Ant falls off once or twice, but eventually gets safely on top of the flowerpot

Right! Fetch the hook.

Glow Worm Would you mind speaking up?

Ant (*shouting*) Fetch the hook!

Red Admiral Sssssh! Slug and company may hear.

Ant (*moderately loudly*) Fetch the hook. It's by my wheelbarrow.

Glow Worm Certainly. (*He gets the hooked rope*)

Ant Throw me the rope end.

Glow Worm starts to throw the hook

No! Not the hook, the rope end.

Glow Worm throws correctly

Now, attach the hook to the foot of the web.

Glow Worm I beg your pardon?

Ant Attach it to the foot.

Glow Worm Are you sure?

Ant Of course.

Glow Worm All right, here goes. (*He puts the hook under his foot*) Ready.

Ant Stand by. Heave.

Ant pulls, and Glow Worm falls over

What's happened?

Glow Worm I don't know. Let's try again. (*He puts the hook back as before*) Ready.
Ant Heave!

Glow Worm falls over again

What's going on?

Glow Worm Are you sure this is right? I keep falling over. I put the hook on my foot as you said.
Ant No, on the foot of the *web*. Then I can lift it up!
Glow Worm Oh! I see.
Ant Be careful, use your hand with the glove on.
Glow Worm Very well. (*He attaches the hook to the web*) Ready.
Ant Right. Heave!

A small hole is made by the web being lifted, with difficulty, by Ant

Once more. Heave!

The web moves higher

It's very heavy, they've stuck stones to the bottom of it, I can't hold on much longer.
Bumble Bee (*who has been watching*) Quick, Glow Worm, pass the other end of the rope through the hole in the top of the flowerpot.
Glow Worm Certainly. (*He goes above the pot to do so*)
Bumble Bee Hang on, Ant.
Ant I'll try.

Glow Worm passes the rope through the hole at the back

Admiral, hold on to it.

Red Admiral does so.

Red Admiral Got it!
Bumble Bee Ladybird, you go through, but *very carefully*, don't touch the web.

Glow Worm holds the web with his gloved hand

SONG: TEN STEPS   17

Red Admiral ⎫	One step, two step, three—
Ladybird ⎬	Soon we'll all be free.
Bumble Bee ⎬	One step, two step, three step, four
Ant ⎭	Softly tread a few steps more

Ladybird escapes and embraces Glow Worm

> Five, six,
> Get out of our fix.
> Seven, eight,
> Escape from our fate.
> Just—
> One, two, three four, five,
> Six, seven, eight, nine, ten—
> Ten steps and we're home again.

Bumble Bee escapes and does a dance of joy

Red Admiral (*Shouts*) Help!

Others   Shhhhh
               Shhhhh
               Don't make a sound.
               For all we know
               Slug and Co.
               May be around.

All   One step, two step, three,
               Soon we'll all be free.

Red Admiral hoists up the web. Ant goes into the pot and takes the rope

> One step, two step, three step, four,
> Softly tread a few steps more.
> Five, six,
> Get out of our fix.
> Seven, eight,
> Escape from our fate.

Red Admiral escapes. Ant drops the rope and web falls

> Just—
> One, two, three, four, five,

Ant escapes through the hole in the pot

> Six, seven, eight, nine, ten—
> Ten steps and we're home again.

Ant collects the glove from Glow Worm and loads the ropes on the barrow.
Glow Worm collects his lantern and the map   **17a**

All exit: Red Admiral, Ladybird, Ant and Glow Worm into the cocoon,
which they close.
From the other side, Slug, Maggot and Greenfly enter, gleefully expecting
to find all four insects caught

They look into the flowerpot, but there is no one there. They separate and look
in different places for them. We hear noises of the Big Ones again as in Act
One—dialogue and then spraying

Man (*off*) Look, there's that horrible slug!
Woman (*off*) And that ghastly greenfly, and that nasty little maggot.
Man (*off*) Take that!

*Not knowing where to run and hide the three panic and end up in the centre of
the stage. As the spray starts they run into the flowerpot, getting tangled up
with the web en route. There are screams of rage as they struggle. The Lights
fade to a Black-out*   **17b**

In the Black-out the flowerpot is struck and Red Admiral opens the cocoon

Scene 6

Red Admiral's home. Day time

*Red Admiral, Ladybird and Ant are finishing a meal—hollyhock or another
flower. On the barrel is a turnip juice jug and a cup, and there are three cups
in the hands of Red Admiral, Ladybird and Ant respectively. Glow Worm is
asleep in the corner.*

Red Admiral Did you see them caught in that web? (*He laughs*) It'll take
them ages to escape.
Ladybird Let's hope so. They must be so angry.
Ant Yes, and when they do escape, where's the first place they'll come?

They all look at one another

Ladybird Here?

Ant nods. There is a knock on the door. All freeze with fear

   Bumble Bee enters

What news?
Bumble Bee (*breathlessly*) They've escaped from the web. Maggot still had
his anti-stick-web gloves on and managed to pull them out.
Ant Hurry scurry, hurry scurry. We must do something!
Red Admiral Where are they now?
Bumble Bee They're plotting again down at Cabbage Patch Corner.
Ladybird What are we going to do?
Bumble Bee Ant, you were on their side once. Can't you think of a plan?
Ant Let me see. Don't hurry scurry me. Yes! I know.
Bumble Bee What?
Ant We must try to catch Slug, Greenfly and Maggot before they destroy
the garden.
Bumble Bee (*enthusiastically*) Yes. (*Realising*) We *know* that, but how?
Red Admiral (*hanging up the map*) Now, Cabbage Patch Corner is *here* and
we are thirty-two degrees to the south-east *here*. If they want to attack,
it won't take them long to get here along this path.
Ant Got it! (*His shout wakes Glow Worm*)
Red Admiral What?

Ant Maggot!

Ladybird (*terrified*) Where?

Ant We catch Maggot first, and what will happen?

Bumble Bee Greenfly will worry about him and start looking for him!

Ant Exactly. Then we catch her.

Ladybird What then?

Ant Slug will look for her, his second-in-command.

Red Admiral And we catch Slug! Brilliant!

Glow Worm (*who has been listening*) But how do we catch young Maggot in the first place?

Red Admiral Don't be so stupid, Glow Worm, we . . . That's a very good point, how *do* we catch Maggot?

Ant Supposing—yes! He's bound to be hungry.

Bumble Bee He's always hungry.

Ladybird And very greedy.

Red Admiral Go on, Ant.

Ant Suppose we lure him with food. Say, a big juicy apple. He'd eat into it, wouldn't he—*right* into it!

Red Admiral Excellent.

Ant (*collecting his barrow*) I'll go and find an apple, if Slug and Co. haven't eaten them all already! Hurry scurry.

Ant exits with his barrow

(*As he goes*) Hurry scurry.

Bumble Bee The problem is, how do we get Maggot to eat into that apple?

Ladybird Couldn't we give it to him as a present?

Bumble Bee No, he might be suspicious.

Red Admiral I know. (*He indicates the Audience*) He might not believe us, but he'd believe *them*.

Red Admiral comes out of the cocoon, followed by Ladybird and Bumble Bee

(*To the Audience*) Would you help us catch Slug and Co.? It's very important. It's for their own good as well as ours. If they continue to eat everything in the garden, then it won't be a nice place for *anyone* to live in, and in the end we'll all starve—including them. We must catch them for everyone's sake. Will you help us? Thank you.

(*He closes the cocoon*) Now, Bumble Bee, you pretend to be Maggot.

Bumble Bee All right. (*To the Audience*) Now, when you see Maggot I expect he'll be very hungry and fancy a wee bite to eat, so you say to him, "Why not have a bite of that apple?" Let's practise that, after three. One, two, three: "*Why not have a bite of that apple?*"

Bumble Bee rehearses the Audience once or twice

Right, now I'll pretend to be Maggot and we'll pretend the apple is over there. Here we go.

Bumble Bee exits, then re-enters imitating Maggot

Ooh! I'm so hungry. I just fancy a nice bite to eat.

Audience (*led by Red Admiral and Ladybird*) Why not have a bite of that apple?

Bumble Bee Ooh! Yes, it looks very juicy. Shall I try it?

Audience Yes!

Bumble Bee All right. (*He mimes nibbling, biting, then climbing into the apple*)

Ladybird Very good. Now I'll pretend to be Greenfly and come on looking for Maggot. I'll say, "Oh dear, that naughty little boy of mine—I've lost him again. Have you seen him?", and you say, "Yes, he's in the apple". Let's just try it. I say, "Have you seen him?", and you say, "Yes, he's in the apple".

Ladybird exits, then re-enters imitating Greenfly

Oh dear, that naughty little boy of mine—I've lost him again—have you seen him?

Audience (*led by Red Admiral and Bumble Bee*) Yes, he's in the apple.

Ladybird Is he really?

Audience Yes.

Ladybird Oh! Thank you. Shall I go and have a look for him?

Audience Yes.

Ladybird All right. (*She mimes going into the apple*)

Red Admiral Top hole! Now then, I'll pretend to be Slug. I expect he'll sail on and say, "Oh dear, I've lost Greenfly, my second-in-command. You haven't seen her, by any chance?", and you say, "Yes, she's in the apple with Maggot". All right? Let's have a practice first. "Yes, she's in the apple with Maggot", after three. One, two, three, "Yes, she's in the apple with Maggot"—good. Let's try it properly.

Red Admiral exits, then re-enters imitating Slug

Oh dear, I've lost Greenfly, my second-in-command. You haven't seen her, by any chance?

Audience (*led by Bumble Bee and Ladybird*) Yes, she's in the apple with Maggot.

Red Admiral Is she?

Audience Yes.

Red Admiral Shall I go and look for her?

Audience Yes.

Red Admiral All right. (*He mimes getting into the apple*) But he'll be so fat after all that eating in the garden that he'll get stuck!

Bumble Bee Should we practise it all again?

Red Admiral Good idea.

Bumble Bee exits and reappears as Maggot

Bumble Bee Ooh I'm hungry. I just fffancy a nice bbbite to eat.

Audience Why not have a bite of that apple?
Bumble Bee Ooh! yes. It looks very juicy. Shall I try it?
Audience Yes.
Bumble Bee All right. (*He mimes nibbling and crawling inside the apple*)

Ladybird exits, and re-enters as Greenfly

Ladybird Oh dear, that naughty little boy of mine—I've lost him again. Have you seen him?
Audience Yes, he's in the apple.
Ladybird Is he really?
Audience Yes.
Ladybird Ooh! Thank you. Shall I go and look for him?
Audience Yes.
Ladybird All right. (*She mimes going into the apple*)

Red Admiral exits, and re-enters as Slug

Red Admiral Oh dear, I've lost Greenfly, my second-in-command. You haven't seen her by any chance?
Audience Yes, she's in the apple with Maggot.
Red Admiral Is she?
Audience Yes.
Red Admiral Shall I go and look for her?
Audience Yes.
Red Admiral All right. (*He mimes getting into the apple and becoming stuck*)

Ant enters with his wheelbarrow and a huge apple and a rope

Ant I've got it! Ooh! It's marvellous, hurry scurry, just like old times.   **18**

They unload the apple and bring it to the centre of the stage

Red Admiral This is admirable! We can't fail.
Ladybird And soon the garden will be back to normal!
Bumble Bee And we can all go back to work.
Ladybird (*looking off*) Oooh! Look out, here comes Maggot.
Red Admiral All right everyone—hide! (*To the Audience*) Don't forget, the whole crew—it's up to you. Get them into the apple!
Bumble Bee (*reminding the Audience*) Why not have a bite of that apple?
Ladybird Yes, he's in the apple.
Red Admiral Yes, she's in the apple with Maggot. Good luck.

Red Admiral, Ant, Ladybird and Bumble Bee all hide behind the cocoon, a flower or a leaf

Maggot enters

Maggot Oooh! I'm so hungry. I just fancy a nice bite to eat.
Audience Why not have a bite of that apple?
Maggot Oooh—yes, it looks very juicy. Shall I try it?
Audience Yes.
Maggot All right. (*He nibbles the apple, bites it, then gets inside*)

Greenfly enters

Greenfly Oh dear, that naughty little boy of mine, I've lost him again. Have
you seen him?
Audience Yes, he's in the apple.
Greenfly Is he really?
Audience Yes.
Greenfly Oh! Thank you. Shall I go and have a look for him?
Audience Yes.
Greenfly All right. (*She goes into the apple*)

Slug enters

Slug Oh dear, I've lost Greenfly, my second-in-command. You haven't seen
her, by any chance?
Audience Yes, she's in the apple with Maggot.
Slug Is she?
Audience Yes.
Slug Shall I go and look for her?
Audience Yes.
Slug All right. (*He starts to get into the apple, but is so fat that he gets stuck*)

Ant and Bumble Bee rush on with the rope and start to tie Slug to the apple, **18a**
going round and round it. Red Admiral and Ladybird watch, delighted.
Suddenly the Lights dim, we hear the back door slam. All stop, look up,
then rush behind the apple. We hear the voices of the Big Ones

Man (*off*) Come on, darling. Let's have a look at the garden.
Woman (*off*) All right, dear, but don't get your feet muddy.
Man (*off*) Oh dear, what a terrible mess! What on earth's happened?
Woman (*off*) It all looks dead. There's no colour in it any more.
Man (*off*) Where's that handsome Red Admiral?
Woman (*off*) And that pretty Ladybird?
Man (*off*) There don't even appear to be any insects to spray any more.
Woman (*off*) What a waste of all your hard work, dear.
Man (*off*) I'm going to give it all up. It's a waste of time. I tell you what,
let's build a garage here instead. The poor old car's getting fed up with
being out in the cold each night.
Woman (*off*) What a good idea, darling—a garage!
Man (*off*) Let's go in and phone up the builders now. A garage—far more
useful than a dead garden.

The door slams. The Lights return to normal. In silence, sobered by the news, Red Admiral, Ladybird, Ant and Bumble Bee release the others and coil up the rope. All except Maggot are very worried

Maggot That's better. It was so hot in there.
All Be quiet.
Red Admiral This could be the end of the garden.
Slug The end of our home.
Ladybird The end of all the happy times we've had.
Greenfly The end of us.

There is a pause

Bumble Bee There must be something we can do.
Ant We'll all have to move.
Maggot (*beginning to cry*) I don't want to move.

There is another pause

Ladybird There's only one solution.
Slug What's that?
Ladybird Well, the Big Ones don't like the garden because it isn't beautiful any more.
Red Admiral Only because Slug and his crew have made it like that.
Greenfly Well, why not? The Big Ones sprayed us . . .
Ladybird Sssh, please. Stop quarrelling. All our lives are in danger, and all you can do is argue.
Bumble Bee Come on, Ladybird, what's the answer?
Ladybird Simple. We must try to make the garden look as beautiful as possible. If we can do that the Big Ones won't want their silly garage.
Ant She's right. Make the garden look the same as it was before.
Red Admiral Not the same—better! What do you say, Slug?
Slug Well . . .
Greenfly Impossible. Why should we do anything for the Big Ones? We hate them.
Maggot Down with the Big Ones!
Greenfly Be quiet. What have they ever done for us? Except spray us.
Slug Wait, Greenfly. They may not have done anything *for* us, but they will do something *to* us if they build their garage.
Ladybird Then you agree?
Slug Well . . .
Red Admiral Come on, let's all join forces—then we won't be fighting *against* one another, but fighting *for* one another.
Ant I think you'd be advised to say yes, Slug.
Slug (*to the Audience*) Should we all join together for the sake of our garden? Should I? Yes? Very well, then. I agree.
Bumble Bee What about you, Greenfly?
Greenfly (*beginning to argue, then thinking better of it*) I . . . Oh! All right.
Maggot Mum, how could you?

Greenfly Listen. Do you want to grow up into a nice strong fly?
Maggot Of course.
Greenfly Then do as your mother tells you. (*She clouts Maggot*)

SONG: INSECTS UNITE!   **19**

Red Admiral ⎫ Insects, unite!
Ladybird ⎪ Insects one and all—
Bumble Bee ⎪ (*The two groups clasp hands*)
Ant   ⎬ Insects, unite—
Slug   ⎪ And answer the call.
Greenfly   ⎪ (*Greenfly and Ladybird embrace, Red Admiral*
Maggot   ⎭ *and Maggot embrace*)

Faced with danger of extinction
Our diff'rences seem small.
United we stand
Divided we fall.

The Big Ones
Are bigger than us
Let's face it,
If they take our home away
We can't replace it.

Insects, unite!
Insects one and all—
Insects, unite—
And answer the call.
Faced with danger of extinction
Our diff'rences seem small.
United we stand
Divided we fall.

Let the breezes blow,
Let the waterfall flow
But most of all—
Let our garden grow.

Insects, unite!
Insects one and all—
Insects, unite—
And answer the call.
Faced with danger of extinction
Our diff'rences seem small.

          United we stand
          Divided we fall.

          Swallow pride and come together;
          We'll fight it hand in hand.
          Divided we fall
          United we stand!

At the end of the song, the music continues in the style of a silent film or ballet. **20**
Red Admiral blows his whistle, miming directions and checking on his map.
Ant is sent off with his wheelbarrow on an errand. Bumble Bee goes off to get
his ladder and begins his rounds once more. Ladybird fetches an acorn cup and
sprinkles water from it. Bumble Bee and Maggot strike the apple. Slug and
Greenfly bring on a large "tin" of fertilizer which they sprinkle around the
flowers, etc. Ant returns with his wheelbarrow, and in it is a packet of seeds
the size of cannon-balls. These are "planted" along the back of the set by the
insects

   The Lights go dark and Glow Worm enters

The night shift continues the work

   Glow Worm checks the work and exits

The Lights return to normal. When the preparations are complete the music
stops

Red Admiral (*to the Audience*) Now, we've all done our share. Perhaps you
   would like to join in. First of all, for the flowers to grow, we need rain,
   but it doesn't look like rain—so p'raps if we make a *noise* like rain they
   might be encouraged to grow—so let's all go "pitter patter pitter patter",
   etc.

The Audience participate

Bumble Bee Now, flowers need warmth too, but there's not very much sun
   today. So let's all blow very hard to make the clouds disappear and the
   sun come out. *Blow!*

The Audience participate. The Lights brighten and give the effect of the sun
appearing

   That's marvellous.
Plug Finally, flowers like to feel surrounded by friendly birds and insects,
   so let's make noises like birds and noises like bees.

The Audience participate, half buzzing, and half making bird noises

Ladybird That's lovely. Now let's do all four again, one after the other, and
   see what happens—"pitter patter pitter patter", "blow", and then chirp-
   ing and then bzzzz.

The Audience participate. Music starts as along the back sunflowers and **20a**
*others are seen to grow, and the garden becomes much more colourful. As the
change finishes we hear the back door open again. Instructed by Red Admiral,
all hide except Ladybird and Red Admiral, who parade themselves in full
view. The Lights dim and shadows form as the Big Ones come out*

Man (*off*) Come on, darling, let's have a last look at the garden.
Woman (*off*) All right, dear, but don't get your feet muddy.
Man (*off*) It's sad to think the garden won't be here much longer.
Woman (*off*) But look, dear—it's changed.
Man (*off*) Good gracious, it's looking much better.
Woman (*off*) I didn't know you'd been working out here again.
Man (*off*) I haven't.
Woman (*off*) Well, that's extraordinary!
Man (*off*) We don't really *need* a garage, do we . . .

Red Admiral moves

Oh look, the red admiral's back!

Ladybird moves

Woman (*off*) And the ladybird!
Man (*off*) Oh! Well then, I'll phone up the builders and tell them we've
changed our minds.
Woman (*off*) Yes.
Man (*off*) I've just thought—maybe that insect spray did it.
Woman (*off*) How do you mean?
Man (*off*) Well, when I used it the garden seemed to die. When I stopped
using it the garden seemed to come to life again.
Woman (*off*) You're right.
Man (*off*) I'll never use that spray again. Come on, let's go in.

*The door slams and the Lights return to normal. All the Insects emerge
cheering*

Bumble Bee We're *all* safe now.
Red Admiral No more garage!
Slug No more spray!
Ladybird So can we all live happily together now?
Greenfly I'll say so! If the Big Ones stop spraying us, we'll stop trying to
fight you!

They all shake hands with one another

   Glow Worm enters

Glow Worm (*sleepily*) What's all the noise about?
Ant We've won, Glow Worm!
Red Admiral No garage—
Slug No spray.
Glow Worm (*falling asleep on his feet*) Oh, that's wonderful! That news is

exciting enough to—wake anybody up. (*He falls, wakes up, and picks himself up*) Oh, I'm so sorry!

Red Admiral Let's celebrate! Here's to a long and happy voyage. God bless all who sail in her . . .

Maggot Hhhhhhhooray!

Greenfly Oh! You've woken up, have you? What have you got to say for yourself?

Maggot Up with the Big Ones!

All (*to the Audience*) *Up with the Big Ones!*

                    SONG: UP WITH THE BIG ONES!   **21**

All (*except the Great Mushroom and Spider*)
                              Up with the Big Ones!

Slug   ⎤
Greenfly   ⎥   We don't hate you any more—
Maggot   ⎥   Up with the Big Ones!
Ant   ⎦

All   No more war!

Slug   ⎤
Greenfly   ⎥   Once you were enemies,
Maggot   ⎥   But now you've made amends.
Ant   ⎦

All   Up with the Big Ones!
                      We're your friends!

     (*to the Audience*)
Ladybird   ⎤   If you've a garden
Red Admiral   ⎬   Take a little bit of care.
Bumble Bee   ⎦   Insects like us are
                      Living there.
                      Try to remember
                      Insects do have feelings too.
                      Be kind to us—
                      And we'll be kind to you.

Maggot   ⎤
Glow Worm   ⎥   (*singing in counterpoint*)
Ant   ⎬   We're your friends,
Slug   ⎥   We're your friends,
Greenfly   ⎦   Friends

All   Be kind to us—
                      And we'll be kind to you.

                          CURTAIN

SONG: REPRISE FOR CURTAIN CALL   **22**

Glow Worm **Bumble Bee** **Red Admiral** **Ladybird**	"The Big Ones like me" etc *(each singing their own version)* *(followed by)* "We're your friends".	*singing together*
Rest of the Company	sing the first section of "Up With the Big Ones" to "We're Your friends", then repeat "We're your friends".	

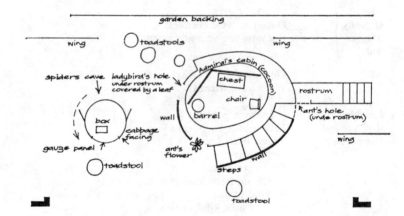

FURNITURE AND PROPERTY LIST

ACT I

On stage: 5 toadstools
In cabbage: box
Behind cabbage: table, hollyhock slice; cabbage cup
In Admiral's cabin: barrel with map on it; chest with compass on it, and 4 cups and turnip juice inside it; chair; bugle behind chair; hook on wall for map
In Ant's hole: wheelbarrow; long rope (for Act II)
In Ladybird's hole: book and pencil; parasol; hand mirror; watering can (acorn)
In front of Ladybird's hole: leaf door; leaf trip
Under rostrum: crayon and leaf banners; broom; stones for web; large pea
On wall of steps: hook for whistle
Around garden: plants, flowers, leaves, acorn cups

Off stage: Lantern, postbag with "Insect News" **(Glow Worm)**
Ladder **(Bumble Bee)**
Compost truck **(Great Mushroom)**
Large flowerpot **(Greenfly, Maggot)**
Stone with hole for Spider's home, with webs, spinning wheel. 3 pairs of anti-web-stick gloves, anti-web-stick spray (SET DURING SCENE 4/5 BLACKOUT)

Personal: **Slug:** walking stick, purple handkerchief
Red Admiral: telescope, pipe and matches, whistle, pocket watch and fob
Ladybird: handkerchief, spectacles
Glow Worm: spectacles
Bumble Bee: bag of pollen balls
Great Mushroom: large handkerchief

ACT II

Strike: Bugle
Whistle from hook and return to Red Admiral

Set: Garden in a "ravaged" state
Stones on bottom of web
Wheelbarrow in Ant hole with long rope, rope with hook, 1 pair of anti-web-stick gloves
Sunflowers and others along back of set to "grow" on cue

Off stage: Toadstool **(Slug, Greenfly)**
Large apple, rope **(Ant)**
"Tin" of fertilizer **(Slug, Greenfly)**
"Packet of seeds" **(Ant)**

LIGHTING PLOT

Property fittings required: nil
Exterior. A Garden. The same scene throughout

ACT I

Dawn

To open	Effect of dim morning light	
Cue 1	**As CURTAIN rises** *Fade up gradually to full daylight*	(Page 1)
Cue 2	**Red Admiral: ". . . on today's agenda, the . . ."** *Light dims: shadow effect for Big Ones*	(Page 8)
Cue 3	**Man: ". . . let's go in."** *Fade up to normal lighting*	(Page 9)
Cue 4	End of "Down with the Big Ones!" reprise *Snap to Black-out*	(Page 14)
Cue 5	At start of Scene 2 *Fade up to night effect on cocoon, with spill over onto site for Great Mushroom*	(Page 14)
Cue 6	**Great Mushroom: "Watch and wiggle."** *Cross-fade to Cabbage*	(Page 19)
Cue 7	**Slug & Co.: "Fight, fight, fight."** *Cross-fade to Great Mushroom*	(Page 20)
Cue 8	**All: "Let our garden grow."** *Fade to Black-out*	(Page 23)
Cue 9	At start of Scene 3 *Slow fade up from dawn to day as Cue 1*	(Page 23)
Cue 10	As **Red Admiral** is followed by flowerpot *Lights dim: shadow effect for Big Ones*	(Page 25)
Cue 11	**Ladybird** and **Bumble Bee** overturn flowerpot *Lights up to normal*	(Page 25)
Cue 12	**All: "Let our garden grow."** *Fade to Black-out*	(Page 25)
Cue 13	At start of Scene 4 *Fade up to normal lighting, with concentration on flowerpot*	(Page 25)
Cue 14	**Ant** and **Maggot** exit *Fade to Black-out*	(Page 27)
Cue 15	At start of Scene 5 *Fade up to spot on **Spider's** home*	(Page 28)
Cue 16	**Spider** exits *Fade to Black-out*	(Page 29)
Cue 17	At start of Scene 6 *Fade up to concentration on cocoon, daylight*	(Page 29)
Cue 18	**Red Admiral** blows bugle *Fade to Black-out*	(Page 31)
Cue 19	At start of Scene 7 *Fade up to normal lighting*	(Page 31)

ACT II

Night

To open	Effect of moonlight, with concentration on flowerpot	
Cue 20	**Bumble Bee:** "Exactly!" *Bring up increased light on cocoon*	(Page 36)
Cue 21	At start of Scene 2 *Cross-fade to Cabbage*	(Page 37)
Cue 22	**Maggot** and **Glow-Worm** exit *Cross-fade to flowerpot, with effect of early dawn*	(Page 39)
Cue 23	**Ant** exits with barrow *Cross-fade to Cabbage*	(Page 41)
Cue 24	At end of "Plotters" song *Fade to black-out*	(Page 43)
Cue 25	As insects emerge from flowerpot *Extend lighting to normal overall*	(Page 46)
Cue 26	As **Slug & Co.** hunt for the others *Lights dim, shadow effect for Big Ones*	(Page 47)
Cue 27	As insects run from spray *Fade to Black-out*	(Page 48)
Cue 28	At start of Scene 6 *Fade up to normal daylight*	(Page 48)
Cue 29	**Slug** is tied to apple *Lights dim, shadow effect for Big Ones*	(Page 52)
Cue 30	**Man:** ". . . more useful than a dead garden." *Lights return to normal*	(Page 52)
Cue 31	As insects repair garden *Fade to night lighting*	(Page 55)
Cue 32	**Glow Worm** exits *Lighting returns to normal daylight*	(Page 55)
Cue 33	As **Audience** "blow" *Bring up bright golden light effect for sun*	(Page 55)
Cue 34	When garden change is complete *Lights dim, shadow effect for Big Ones*	(Page 56)
Cue 35	**Man:** ". . . let's go in." *Return to Cue 33*	(Page 56)

EFFECTS PLOT

ACT I

Cue 1	As Curtain rises *Dawn chorus of birds*	(Page 1)
Cue 2	**Red Admiral:** ". . . on today's agenda, the . . ." *Door opening*	(Page 8)
Cue 3	**Man:** "Take that!" *Spray effect*	(Page 9)
Cue 4	**Man:** ". . . let's go in." *Door slam*	(Page 9)
Cue 5	The **Great Mushroom** arrives *Loud sneeze over speaker*	(Page 18)
Cue 6	**Great Mushroom:** "Get up, get up—a . . ." *Loud sneeze over speaker*	(Page 18)
Cue 7	Lights come up on **Great Mushroom** *Loud sneeze over speaker*	(Page 18)
Cue 8	As Lights dim for Big Ones *Door slam*	(Page 25)
Cue 9	**Red Admiral** exits *Spray effect*	(Page 25)
Cue 10	**Ladybird** and **Bumble Bee** overturn flowerpot *Spray effect stops. Door slam*	(Page 25)

ACT II

Cue 11	As Lights dim for Big Ones *Door slam, followed by spray effect*	(Page 47)
Cue 12	As Lights dim for Big Ones *Door slam*	(Page 52)
Cue 13	**Man:** ". . . more useful than a dead garden." *Door slam*	(Page 52)
Cue 14	As Lights dim for Big Ones *Door slam*	(Page 53)
Cue 15	**Man:** ". . . let's go in." *Door slam*	(Page 56)

MADE AND PRINTED IN GREAT BRITAIN BY
LATIMER TREND & COMPANY LTD, PLYMOUTH
MADE IN ENGLAND